Kenya and The Terrible Tornado Toilet

By Lisa Hook Bell

Lyfe Publishing
Publishers Since 2012
Published by Lyfe Publishing LLC
Lyfe Publishing, 10800 Nautica Place, White Plains MD 20695

Congress Cataloging in Publications Data
Bell, Lisa Hook
Kenya & The Terrible Tornado Toilet/Lisa Hook Bell
ISBN: 978-1-957333-21-2
(Fictitious Character)–Fiction
Tampa, Florida
Kenya & The Terrible Tornado Toilet–Fiction
Printed in the United States of America
1 2 3 4 5 6 7 8 9 10
Book design by Atiyya Nadirah

Dedication

This book is lovingly dedicated to my beloved parents, Julian and Martha Hook, and my little brother, Marquis. They deeply enriched my life and childhood with constant inspiration and cherished memories. To my amazing husband, Henry, for his unconditional love, guidance and support and for being my biggest fan. Also to our remarkable sons, Julian, Trey and Marquis and to my loving daughter-in-law, Sasha and our beautiful grandchildren Zionah, Nekhali, Amara and Aziah for their constant love and encouragement! Much gratitude and appreciation to them and all my friends and family for always believing in me and encouraging me to believe in myself.

Acknowledgement

Thank you for your loving and much appreciated support with Kenya and The Terrible Tornado Toilet.

Mary Freeney
Angela Holton
Renitta Knight Lundy
Betty Bell (Ma Bell)
Dannie Stewart
Elaine Ramirez
Charlene Dorsey
Darlene Daggs
Desiree Washington
Vendetta and Ray DeSouza
Melissa Jones
Michelle Stone
Dori Blanc
Michele Vinson
Mickey Morrison
Sammecia Bagley
Rangelique McCray
Edrina Hammond
Drs. James and Cher Pruitt
Meikah Stokely
Sharice and Alonzo Barnes
Attorney Clinton Paris
Barbara Barnes
Elizabeth Simpson
Olivia Baxley

Additionally, my extremely talented illustrator, Atiyya Nadirah, my knowledgeable and dedicated publisher, Gerald C. Anderson, Sr. and a host of others. Your dedication and support mean more than words can express. Thank you.

Dear Parents, Guardians, and Educators,

Thank you for your interest in selecting this book for your child or children.

Kenya and the Terrible Tornado Toilet is the first installment from the Kenya Lancer Series.

Every book in this series stresses the importance of having good character and learning valuable lessons. This lesson is expressed in a positive, lighthearted, and humorous format through the eyes of a young, sassy kindergartner. The books are designed to help your child or children identify with the character and laugh out loud.

I'd be remiss as a former educator, if I didn't take the time to stress the importance of actively engaging children into the wonderful world of Reading.

Regardless, if they are simply listening to you read or enjoying the book independently, it's imperative that you ask them a variety of questions throughout the story to increase comprehension.

Can't think of any questions, don't worry, I've got you!

To assist parents, guardians and educators, I have created an instructional guide to help you out. It's a digital download that is absolutely FREE when you sign up for my newsletter.

Go to my website, listed below, to find out more and to see some adorable Kenya Lancer merchandise.

JOIN THE PARTY!

Please go to my website (www.lisahookbell.com) and sign up for my newsletter!

- You'll have access to the free instructional guide
- Receive helpful tips to enhance Reading.
- Get advice for authors, young and old.
- Win cool prizes.
- Get inside info about Kenya.
- Browse and purchase Kenya Lancer's adorable Merchandise.
- Be the first to know when Kenya's next book is coming out.

Thank you again for your interest and support and welcome to the Kenya Lancer family! Have a Kenya Kind of Day! ☺

Table of Contents

Chapter 1 – Introduction

Hi, my name is Kenya Lancer. I was born in Tampa, Florida and I actually still live there now. I'm 5 years old and I just graduated from Pre K! Now, I always thought that when someone graduated from school, that meant they were done, but apparently I have some more learning to do. I learned that fancy word from my mom.

My parents just told me that I must start something called "Tend Your Garden" soon. Now, I don't really care for vegetables that much, so I really don't know why I have to go to school to learn about growing a garden, but my mom says that I don't really have a choice.

So, I guess that's what I'll be doing starting next week. I sure do hope that it's an indoor kind of garden, 'cause Florida is hotter than sweatpants at the beach this time of year. I heard my grandpa say that once! Well "Tend Your Garden," here I come!

Chapter 2 – Future Job

Newsflash! I was just informed that I will not be a farmer after all! I'm going to something called Kindergarten, and it's the grade you go to after Pre–K. I don't know why I have to go; everyone is always telling me that they can't believe how many big words I already know and how smart I already am, but apparently that's not enough for these people!

And guess what else? My mom told me I actually have YEARS of school left! I have 13 YEARS in regular school and then 4 or 5 more years in something called college!

Are you serious people? I'll probably be a gray haired old lady, like both of my grandmas by then! Hey, don't tell them I said that, ok?

The good news is, I heard that once I get there, they'll let me play outside every single day and they'll feed me a delicious lunch too. So if that's my future job until I retire, I guess I can handle that!

Chapter 3 — Australia

I have a big, mean sister and her name is Maya. She just turned 11, and she is, how do I say this... well, she's a snitch! No really, all she does is tattletale on me to our parents.

Sometimes when our parents are busy, they'll ask her to watch me and that's exactly what she does! She watches every move I make and then she runs to tell our parents what I did wrong or what I said that was "in the propriate!"

I think that's her favorite word in the whole wide world! It means something that you should not say or do, at least not when your mean big sister is around! Did I mention that she's a snitch?

Anywho, Maya is starting something called Middle School next week. It should be called Mental School if she's going there! I'm not sure what it is, I just hope it's in the middle of Australia! Then maybe she'll have to live there and that would be fine with me. 'Cause it's awfully hard to tattletale from that far away!

Chapter 4 – Team Uniforms

Today we're shopping for school clothes and guess what? I'll be wearing uniforms this year! Hey, I didn't even know that I was going to be on a team! I'm so excited and I hope it's going to be a basketball team, 'cause I'm really good at basketball. Especially when I stand under the basket... and no one blocks me! I'll probably be the star of the team!

Anywho, when we got to the store, I could hardly wait to get my uniforms! But then I noticed that Mom was walking right past all the basketball stuff. "Hey Mom, my uniforms should be over here!" I shouted. "No, they're over here!" she replied as she headed to some plain, boring looking clothes.

She was looking at some plain white shirts and some tannish colored shorts and skirts. Mom shared I could also wear red shirts, which is my favorite color, but these clothes were not very attractive, I tell you!

Are you kidding? This is my new uniform! # BORING! No bright, pretty colors? No polka dots, flowers or colorful unicorns on the shirts?

Who is on the fashion design team at this school? I'm so upset right now, 'cause apparently, somebody needs to watch a few episodes of Project Runaway!!!

Chapter 5 — Dream Crusher

Welp, Mom is a dream crusher! She just explained to me that I really needed to get over my "little attitude" because I had to wear the school uniform, even if I didn't like it. In fact, everybody has to wear the same exact uniform, every single day! That is so not exciting! I mean, how will they even tell us apart?

And guess what else? I'm not going to be on anybody's basketball team either! Mom really is a dream crusher! And of course, my mean big sister Maya, thought the whole thing was just so funny! "You actually thought that you were going to wear basketball uniforms to school and play on a team!" she laughed loudly, holding her stomach! She really gets on my nerves!

Nothing about this whole situation was funny to me! I really don't care for these boring school uniforms, and I really don't think kids should have to suffer just because someone else has poor fashion taste! You know, I don't think I'm going to like this Kindergarten place after all, not one little bit!

Chapter 6 – Not Fair at All

Well, tomorrow is the first day of school and I'm still not feeling very excited about my new uniforms. They just seem so boring and they're really stifling the fashionista in me! (I heard that on that Project Runaway show, that the people at my school should have been watching!)

Mom made me try one on, so we could see how I'm going to look tomorrow. She really tried to make the uniform look cuter by buying me lots of colorful bows for my hair and lacey white socks to wear with my new shiny black shoes, but it still was not very attractive.

"So, what do you think?" Mom asked excitedly. "Well... I guess you tried." I sighed as I looked at myself in the mirror. I got the feeling that she didn't like my comment very much.

Speaking of not liking something, my sister Maya has been extra "anoising" all week! Did I tell you that she gets to wear regular people's clothes to school? That's not fair at all!

She bragged about it every time she saw me, and she tried on her new outfits like 50 thousand times! Ugh, I'm so over her! She kept prancing into my room with a new outfit on, singing out "What do you think of this one?" and I kept yelling for her to stay out, but she didn't listen.

Finally, I told her what I really thought about her ugly new outfits, and she ran to tell Mom and Dad. I told you that she was a snitch! Well, apparently what I said was "in the propriate" and I spent my last night of summer freedom in time out. Life is so unfair sometimes and I'm still hoping that my sister's new school is in West Australia!

Chapter 7 – First Day of School

Today is the first day of school and I'm not feeling that good at all. I told Mom that my tummy felt kind of sickish and that I probably needed to stay home and rest, but she was not in an understanding mood. She said that I probably just had butterflies in my stomach.

What!!! So now she thinks I'm a frog or something. What would make her think that I've been munching on flies! That's just nasty! Although, I ate a gnat once, but that was by accident! So don't judge me!

Finally, Mom explained that she just meant that my tummy felt upset because I was feeling nervous about school. Well, why didn't she just say that in the first place? I don't need extra stress in my life, you know!

Anywho, I felt much better after I ate breakfast and got dressed. And guess what? My new uniform didn't look as bad as I thought! I added my sparkly pink and purple unicorn necklace and a few bracelets, and it really brought my outfit to life.

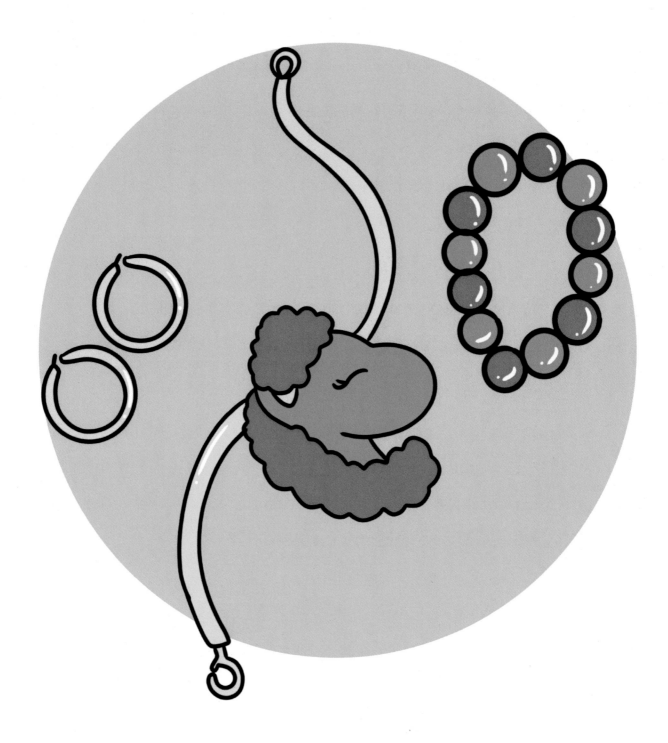

Well, a lady should always "accessorize to maximize." I heard that on a Macy's commercial last week. Mom also said that I can wear the necklace, if my new teacher says that it's ok and I really hope she does!

I also hope that I like this Kindergarten thing. My parents took me to school, and while Dad drove, Mom kept turning around and telling me about how much fun it's going to be.

I really hope that I can trust what she says. I mean, she wasn't very clear about that whole butterfly conversation we had earlier, but I guess I can believe her. I know one thing, if it's not fun, I might be the one moving! I'll be moving to West Africa and that's that!

Chapter 8 – My New Teacher

Well, I met my new teacher today, and she is amazing!! She's very pretty and nice and guess what else? She looks just like me! Well, she doesn't have short legs and ponytail puffs, but her skin is brown, just like mine! I've never had a teacher like that in my whole entire career.

Don't get me wrong, I loved my Pre–K teacher, but this one kind of makes me feel like she's my auntie or something. Her name is Ms. Lockett and guess what else, she said that I can wear my unicorn necklace and that she really liked it! I just love a woman with style!

Ms. Lockett greeted us at the door with a big, friendly smile and she already knew my name. She introduced herself and said she had been waiting to meet me all summer long. I hugged her real tight, because I was really glad to meet her too!

Before she went to talk with my parents, she walked me to my new desk. It already had a nametag with my name on it, along with some fancy coloring sheets and a box of brand new colorful crayons.

The classroom was decorated with bright, colorful posters, billions of cute books, and a nice cozy rug with a huge rocking chair. The other kids that were already there seemed very nice as they quietly colored their worksheets. I was really excited, 'cause this teacher seemed to really know what she was doing.

Mom and Dad waved goodbye, and I didn't even feel nervous anymore. I waved back and smiled to myself, 'cause I think Kindergarten is going to be a fun place after all!

Chapter 9 – The Problem

Newsflash! Kindergarten is the funnest place ever! We sing silly songs, learn about letter sounds, cool words, and big kid Math. We also get to color and listen to Ms. Lockett read us amazing stories on the fluffy rug as she sits in her huge rocking chair. That's my favorite part of the day!

My other favorite part of the day is going outside to play on the playground! It's awesome out there and we get to play there every single day, unless it's raining. I can definitely do this for the next 13 years with no problem!

Speaking of problems, there is one big, horrible, scary problem in my kindergarten class... and it's called the terrible tornado toilet! No really, it's not like regular toilets, which I don't have any problems with at all.

This one is the loudest toilet that I've ever heard. It has the suction power of a thousand vacuum cleaners, and it almost sucked me and my soul down that little hole today. Honestly, I was almost gone and never to be heard from again!

The whole terrible experience happened today after story time! After using the restroom, I went to flush that little jiggly thing on the side and that's when the trouble started!

Suddenly, the toilet growled and grumbled like a wild, hungry animal, and the ground shook and trembled under my feet. My heart began to race even faster as the sound grew louder and louder and the water swirled around faster and faster until it became a raging tornado!

I could feel the powerful suction of it pulling me toward it! I ran to the door and held onto the doorknob with both hands and prayed that it wouldn't get me. I felt the need to stop, drop, and roll, but I think that's only when you're on fire. I learned about that in Pre–K, but back to the tornado toilet!

It was shaking, grumbling, and sucking; the swirling seemed to go on forever as my ponytail puffs flew out behind me. I really didn't think that I was going to survive! It was the most terrifying experience of my whole entire career and then suddenly, everything was quiet!!

Chapter 10 – The Terrible Tornado Toilet

My legs were still quivering as I slowly opened my eyes and looked around to make sure none of me had been sucked down into that little hole.

Luckily, I was all there in one piece. Apparently, I must have screamed a little, because Ms. Lockett knocked on the door and asked if I was ok! Now, where was she when the tornado toilet was trying to get me?

I wiped my eyes, because my allergies started acting up or something and I told her that I was ok. She then informed me I needed to come back and join the class, so I washed my trembling hands and returned to my seat.

It took a long time for my heart to slow down again. I had told Ms. Lockett I was fine, but I really wasn't. I was truly "tramalized" and I decided to never, ever use that terrible tornado toilet ever again!

It took me all morning to calm down, but I finally recovered from my toilet trauma! My teacher started teaching us about something really cool called Science and we learned about different kinds of animals and their cute little babies.

The lesson was really fun, and it made me forget all about my toilet troubles. That is, until later that afternoon!

Chapter 11 – Not Again

Ms. Lockett took us out to the playground after lunch and we had a wonderful time. I ran around with my new friends so much that I began to get hot and thirsty, so I ran to the water fountain and drank, and drank, and drank.

Afterwards, we returned to class and began coloring an animal worksheet, when I suddenly realized that I was having another problem. And it's called, I had to go to the bathroom again... and really bad! "Oh no, not again!" I thought to myself.

I tried to ignore the feeling for as long as I could, but I knew that I'd better go soon or there was going to be a situation and all my new friends would laugh at me. I suddenly got up and ran into the bathroom, as fast as the wind!

The heavy door slammed behind me, as I stood staring with wide eyes at the toilet monster in front of me. It seemed to be even bigger than before! I really didn't want to risk being sucked away by the tornado toilet again, I might not be lucky enough to survive this time. But I was running out of time and I really had to go. I took a deep breath, and my heart began to race again as I realized I had to face the terrible tornado toilet once again! I had no choice!

Chapter 12 – Another Choice

I was terrified as I gazed around the bathroom. Then I noticed a nice, little blue plastic garbage can sitting in the corner. I felt relief as I realized I had another choice and I had found a solution to my problem. I felt even more relieved after I finished 'cause I almost didn't make it in time.

I put lots of tissue in the garbage can to cover up the evidence and I smiled as I washed my hands. I was so proud of myself and the rest of the day was amazing!

We watched a wonderful video about letter sounds and Ms. Lockett let us write stories in our new writing journals. I wrote a story about a mean, scary monster who gets beat up by a strong, brave superhero girl! It was a great story, if I say so myself!

I didn't have to use the restroom again before the end of the day, but it felt wonderful knowing that when I needed to go, it wasn't going to be a problem for me anymore. I now had a secret solution and Kindergarten was once again a wonderful place to be!

Chapter 13 – Teacher Trouble

As I entered the classroom the next morning, I could tell something was wrong. Ms. Lockett didn't seem as happy to see us as usual and she said that she needed to have a serious discussion with us after we said the "pledge of the legents."

She looked very serious as she talked to us about how we all were big, responsible kindergartners. I hoped she would get to the point soon, so I could finish coloring my morning worksheet, but then she mentioned something about a horrible discovery in the bathroom and that got my attention!

Apparently, the school custodian, Mr. Keystone, is also a snitch. He told her he discovered that someone had used the little blue garbage can in the restroom as a toilet. I nervously glanced around the room to see if anyone suspected it was me.

44

All the kids were looking surprised and disgusted, so I made my face look the same. "That's awful!" I shouted. Ms. Lockett agreed and continued her discussion about what a garbage can is really for and us not being babies, but I noticed she seemed to talk mostly to the boys. She seemed to think that one of the boys did it! Whew, I was in the clear!

So later that day, after I used my not – so – secret blue plastic toilet again, I wasn't even worried. After all, the teacher thought it was one of the five boys in our class and by the time she figured it all out, it would be time for the summer again. So, I wasn't in trouble. Life was good, and I was happy. At least until the very next day!

Chapter 14 – Garbage Can Blues

Ms. Lockett looked upset again the next morning. She talked on and on about being disappointed about the bathroom situation. I shook my head and looked at the five nervous little boys. Ms. Lockett even talked about calling parents and trips to the principal's office. I was so glad that she didn't know the truth.

Later that morning, I had to make my little trip to the bathroom, and it was only after I closed the door behind me that I realized that there was a big problem. My little blue plastic secret garbage can was GONE! I looked everywhere for it. Even behind the scary tornado toilet, but it was nowhere to be found. Who moved it?

But what was worse, now I had to go really, really bad. "Oh no, oh no" I whined. I jumped onto the tornado toilet right in time! WHEW!

As I sat there with my heart racing, I whispered to myself so I wouldn't have a "pantic attack." "I'm a big girl and I can do this." Then I started thinking, "Hey, I'm not afraid of using the toilet. I'm just afraid of flushing it!"

"So, I just wouldn't flush anymore!" What a great idea! That way, the next person to use the bathroom who wasn't afraid of being sucked away could flush it when they came in and the world would be at peace. Problem solved!

Chapter 15 – Mean Girl Mallory

I washed my hands and skipped back to my seat, quite happy with myself and everything was great! That is until this mean bossy girl named Mallory decided she needed to use the bathroom.

I already knew she wasn't a very nice person. One the first day of school Mallory laughed at me when my crayon box fell off my desk and all of my new colorful crayons fell out on the floor. And the worst part was, my favorite red crayon broke in two!

Mallory laughed and laughed, and then my allergies started acting up again. Ms. Lockett fussed at Mallory for being mean and a really nice girl named Angela came over to help me pick up my crayons, without me even asking. And guess what else? When she saw how upset I was about my broken red crayon, she gave me hers. Now that's what I call being a nice citizen! She's my new best friend!

Anywho, Mallory, who is not my best friend, is also a snitch! 'Cause right after she went into the bathroom, she came right back out and announced to the whole entire class "Ewwww, Kenya Lancer didn't even flush the toilet!" I was so mad and embarrassed! "Mind your own business, you big old snitch!" I yelled out!

Apparently, that was "in the propriate" and I had to apologize to Mallory and the entire class. But I didn't have to flush the terrible tornado toilet! Ms. Lockett flushed it and had a quiet talk with Mallory about yelling in the classroom. It wasn't the best day of kindergarten for me, but it wasn't the worst either.

Chapter 16 – Best Friend, Angela

The next day started off pretty good. Until I heard that mean girl, Mallory had told everyone that if anybody (meaning me), didn't flush the toilet after using it, they should go tell the teacher. 'Cause doing that was rude and disgusting.

Well, I think she's rude and disgusting, so I stuck my tongue at her. She told everybody not to play with me when we went outside, but guess who still played with me... my new best friend, Angela!

She wanted to play tag, but I didn't really feel up to it because I had nothing to drink all day, and you know why! I was feeling kind of tired and a bit "de hybrated." So, we just sat under a tree and talked.

Angela really is a sweet person and a very nice friend. After we returned to class, my throat was so dry that I could hardly stand it.

Finally, I had to get a drink from the water fountain and then, of course, while I was adding more cool details to my monster story, I had to go you know where... the bathroom! For as long as I could, I tried to ignore the feeling! I tried to cross my legs and stay busy writing my story. I even tried to think of dry things like sidewalk chalk sprinkles that get in your throat, like the hot desert and even my mom's dry Monday night meatloaf, but nothing worked!

The next thing I knew, I began to do a fast, little dance by my desk and not a cool TIkTok dance either! At the last minute, I ran as fast as the wind into the restroom and slammed the door shut! I sure miss that little, blue plastic garbage can right now!

Chapter 17 – The Worst Day of Kindergarten

As I stared at the terrifying tornado toilet I continued to do my weird marching dance. I didn't know what to do, my blue plastic secret toilet was gone, and I'd get in big trouble for not flushing, thanks to that big mouth, mean girl, Mallory! I was out of solutions and apparently out of time, because suddenly, a big, horrible problem started happening!

This problem went down both of my legs and soaked my fluffy white socks. It even ran into my shiny new black shoes and some got on the back of my new tan skirt too! It was the Worst Day of Kindergarten Ever!

This time my allergies were worse than ever, and I couldn't help but cry and cry. I tried to do it silently so nobody could hear me, but it was hard... really, really hard!

Next, I tried to dry my tears and my soaked shoes, socks, and skirt with paper towels. I even ran around in circles again and again to see if it would help me dry off faster, but it didn't seem to work at all. Then there was a knock at the door, and I froze like a statue!

Ms. Lockett must have noticed how long I had been in the bathroom. That lady seems to notice everything, I tell you! She gently knocked again and asked if I was ok. I quickly told her I was, but I really wasn't.

I really, really wasn't!

Chapter 18 – More Teacher Trouble

I waited until I heard Ms. Lockett walk away from the bathroom door and I slowly opened the door and peeked out. When I saw she was sitting back down to work with her Reading group again, I rushed out of the door and quickly threw the wet paper towels into the garbage can, which was now kept outside of the restroom. And I raced to sit down at my desk before she could see me. Whew, I just made it!

Ms. Lockett glanced up and smiled warmly at me, and I smiled and waved at her so she wouldn't be concerned. Now, if my clothes would just hurry up and dry before dismissal, everything would be just fine.

Suddenly, Ms. Lockett ended her first Reading group and told those students to return to their seats to finish their class work. I started praying hard that she didn't call my Reading group next. But then something worser happened. She actually started slowly walking towards my desk.

My heart began to beat faster! Ms. Lockett must have seen something! I told you she doesn't miss anything! Her name should really be Ms. Look–At, 'cause she sees everything!

She quietly bent down next to me and asked again if everything was alright. I told her yes and tried to look like I was too busy doing my work to talk to her. That's when I noticed her looking down at my soggy wet socks.

"Oh No!" I thought to myself. I think teachers must be detectives too.

Chapter 19 – A Trip to the Office

Ms. Lockett whispered in my ear as she gently put her hand on my shoulder. "Did you have an accident in the bathroom, Kenya?" I looked down at the ground and slowly nodded! Allergies again! Ms. Lockett handed me a tissue and went to whisper on the classroom phone. Soon, another teacher magically appeared at our door and came in as Ms. Lockett walked back over to me.

She took off her very own sweater and tied it around my waist and then she took me by my hand and the two of us walked to the front office together to call my mom. She said that I wasn't in trouble, but I needed to get out of those wet clothes. She really is a nice teacher!

Mom came to the school with dry clothes for me and I told her and Ms. Lockett all about the terrible tornado toilet and what had happened to me over the last few days. They were both pretty understanding, although my mom looked a little embarrassed when I shared the part about the little blue plastic garbage can.

I went home early that day, and even though I wasn't in trouble, I still felt kind of bad. What if everyone in my class found out what happened? What would Mallory say? My mom kept talking to me about overcoming fears and stuff like that, but I just wanted to get home so I could Google how much it costs to fly to Africa.

Chapter 20 – Our Little Secret

The next morning, I was really nervous about going back to school and I tried to act like I was feeling too sick to go, but apparently my acting skills are not that great. Mom took me to school anyway, but she gave me a big hug at the door and reminded me to be brave.

I slowly opened the classroom door, and everything seemed pretty normal. Nobody laughed or said anything mean. I don't think they even knew what happened at all. Apparently, Ms. Lockett is not a snitch, and she seemed as happy to see me as usual. I love that lady!

And guess what else? She's a problem solver too! She had a plan for me to get over my fear of the terrible tornado toilet. First, she asked our custodian, Mr. Keystone, to fix the toilet so it wouldn't flush so loud and strong. We call him Mr. Keys because he has like 5 million, billion keys on his keychain.

Anywho, Mr. Keys is my hero, and so is Ms. Lockett! She gave me a little brown rope I could wrap around the door handle and hold on to while the toilet flushed. At least until I felt braver about not being sucked down into the toilet and it worked!

What a great idea! We kept the little rope hidden in a small school box behind the little blue garbage can. Yes, the garbage can was back. And the whole thing was our little secret... me, and my wonderful, non—snitching kindergarten teacher!

Chapter 21 – Time to Celebrate

It took about a week or two, but I could finally use the restroom without using the little brown rope! Yay, I was so proud of myself! To celebrate, I took that old rope and flushed it right out of there! I clapped and clapped as it swirled away and disappeared down the little hole.

I was so happy and excited until I noticed a strange noise and then the water in the toilet got higher and higher. It went all the way up to where the seat was, and it didn't go back down.

Well, it looks like kindergarten is going to have a lot of challenges and I might just be heading to Africa after all!

Kenya and the Terrible Tornado Toilet

Kenya Lancer's Lessons

Hey Friends,

It's me, Kenya. What lesson did you learn in this story?

I learned that we all have fears, it's ok and it's normal. That fear may not even be scary to everyone else, but it's scary to you and it is important that you stand tall, be brave, and face whatever you're afraid of. You may find out that it's not as scary as you thought it was!

Getting over this fear may take a while and you may need some help, but that's ok, you can do it! I know you can!

Anywho, don't forget to look for my next book. You won't believe what happens to me there! Until then, always choose kindness, believe in yourself, and have a Kenya Kind of Day!

Love Your Friend,

Kenya🖤

Made in the USA
Monee, IL
06 December 2022

19683021R00048

SIMPLE TO CREATE, GOURMET ON THE PLATE

Come and join me on my journey.

Ricky K

Simply GOURMET

BY RIVKY KLEIMAN

PHOTOGRAPHY BY MOSHE WULLIGER

SIMPLE TO CREATE, GOURMET ON THE PLATE

RivkyK

**A complete culinary collection
for all your kosher cooking**

Published by ARTSCROLL / SHAAR PRESS
4401 Second Avenue / Brooklyn, NY 11232 / (718) 921-9000 www.artscroll.com

Distributed in Israel by SIFRIATI / A. GITLER
POB 2351 / Bnei Brak 51122 / Israel / 03-579-8187

Distributed in Europe by LEHMANNS
Unit E, Viking Business Park, Rolling Mill Road Jarrow, Tyne and Wear, NE32 3DP / England

Distributed in Australia and New Zealand by GOLDS WORLD OF JUDAICA
3-13 William Street / Balaclava, Melbourne 3183, Victoria / Australia

Distributed in South Africa by KOLLEL BOOKSHOP
Northfield Centre / 17 Northfield Avenue / Glenhazel 2192 Johannesburg, South Africa

ISBN-10: 1-4226-2318-1 / ISBN-13: 978-1-4226-2318-3

Printed in Canada

ACKNOWLEDGMENTS

First and foremost, I am humbled and grateful to *Hakadosh Baruch Hu* for the abundant goodness that He continually bestows upon me.

My parents raised me to reach for the stars and to believe that nothing was impossible to achieve. Thank you for encouraging and believing in me. I am who I am because of you and the wonderful example you set.

Special thanks to *my in-laws* for always standing by me and being an inspiration to the family.

To all *my "sibs"* and *their "fams"*: "All for one and one for all" has always been our motto. (I thank Hashem every day for my most amazing family.)

I thank my talented food editor, *Chanie Nayman* and extended *Mishpacha* personnel for being friends and family. You are the most amazing creative "foodie"team, and you make my work simply fun.

Rabbi Gedaliah Zlotowitz is a true visionary and trailblazer in the kosher culinary world and beyond. Together with your incredible ArtScroll team, you continue to perpetuate the legacy of your illustrious father *zt"l*.

To my editor par excellence, the fabulous *Felice Eisner*, your command of the English language never ceases to amaze. Your attention to every detail ensures that the final product is close to perfect.

Tova Ovits and *Judi Dick*, your proofreading and editing not only caught typos but also helped clarify the instructions so that they are more easily understood.

Devorah Cohen, your creative talents make each and every page in this book truly eye-catching.

Eli Kroen, your input enhanced the appearance of the cover, and your experienced eye is much appreciated.

Renee Muller, food stylist par excellence, for your encouragement and hand-holding throughout this incredible journey. *Moshe Wulliger*, iconic food photographer, who managed to make hard work fun. Working on this project with both of you has been a magical experience. So honored to be part of this "dream team."

Chaya Faigy Uhr, Raizy Yurowitz, and *Marni Levy*, I so appreciate knowing that I could always count on you.

Miriam Pascal and *Leah Schapira*, you shared your time, talents, and expertise without hesitation, and for that I am truly grateful.

Hindy Kleiman and *Esther Leah Sandhaus*, thank you for going above and beyond merely putting words and thoughts on paper.

Colorush Marketing (www.colorush.com), this magnificent cover and layout design are testament to your incredible talent.

Special thanks to *The Fishing Line* of Lakewood, NJ: one taste and you'll be "hooked," and to *Epstein's Meat* of Lakewood, NJ, whose meat is always a "cut" above the rest.

Special shout-out to *Sari Rubnitz* and *Meesh Pasternak*: your keen and creative eyes are always appreciated both in the kitchen and on social media.

Last but certainly not least, thanks to my *husband*, *children*, and *grandchildren*. You are my world! Thank you for being there for me through thick and thin. For being my taste testers and critics and always being great sports about it. I truly could not have done this without you.

TABLE OF CONTENTS

DESSERTS

BAKED GOODS

My Team of Taste Testers:
Esti Adler • Tova Beer • Nechama Beren • Pnina Bravmann • Huvie Eisenreich •
Chani Follman • Shoshi Jakob • Hindy Kleiman • Shana Kleiman • Zisi Kleiman •
Michal Mammon • Tobie Nussbaum • Gitty Pultman • Sari Rubnitz • Baila Sandhaus •
Esther Leah Sandhaus • Leah Schamovic • Chanie Schlisselfeld • Shayna Strassman •
Yael Straz • Yael Taub • Hadassah Weinberg • Chantzy Weinstein • Raizy Yurowitz

AUTHOR'S PREFACE

To my readers,

As far back as I can remember, my mother and I were a dynamic duo, whipping up a storm in the kitchen for every Shabbos and Yom Tov. I was always excited to be her sous chef. My mother attended culinary school before it was en vogue, and her professional training definitely inspired my cutting edge and gourmet style. Thankfully, by the time I married, the kitchen was a familiar domain.

Teaching was another of my passions. I taught young children in the classroom for two decades. My love of teaching and the kitchen were merged when my friends and I embarked on a mammoth project that resulted in the wildly popular *Bais Yaakov Cookbooks*. This undertaking gave me the opportunity to teach others how to bring delicious Shabbos, Yom Tov and everyday meals into their homes. The publicity resulting from the first cookbook release and the rave reviews it received were followed by the invitation from *Mishpacha* magazine to join their team. Since joining *Mishpacha* I have had countless requests to publish a cookbook; this book is the result of those requests.

This cookbook is about using my **Simply Gourmet** style to turn out meals that are delicious, sophisticated, and most of all, very doable.

Writing this book has been a labor of love. I hope you enjoy these recipes as much as I enjoyed developing them for you and they become staples at your table.

INTRODUCTION

Life has become so fast paced that one aspect of my goal is to alleviate the stress of feeding families in record time. In these pages you will find some recipes that include a "simple supper" icon in the far left corner of the page.

To be dubbed a "simple supper," a recipe meets very strict criteria:

- Prep time must be no longer than 10 minutes total.

- The food must be ready to serve in less than an hour.

Some "simple supper" recipes that fit these guidelines can have dinner on the table within 30 minutes!

To easily identify the level of difficulty of each dish, look for the number and type of utensils pictured:

A spoon means that the recipe is simple and beginner level.

A spoon and a knife indicate a recipe requiring intermediate skill and somewhat more prep time.

A spoon, knife, and fork signify a lengthy process or a more advanced level of expertise.

In a Pinch ...

While my preference in recipes is always...

FRESH GARLIC: if you don't have fresh on hand, frozen crushed garlic is a handy substitute. Replace each garlic clove with 1 cube frozen crushed garlic.

CHICKEN BROTH: if you don't have broth on hand, water with consommé powder will work well. Substitute 1 cup broth (any type) with 1 cup water + 1 tsp consommé powder.

FRESH HERBS: If you don't have any on hand, dried herbs are a great help. Substitute 1 Tbsp fresh herbs with 1 tsp dried herbs. (The ratio is always 3:1). Frozen herb cubes are also useful. However, the flavor is much more concentrated, so the ratio is different. Substitute ¼ cup fresh herbs with 3 frozen herb cubes.

Substitutions

In my recipes, I tried to use ingredients that are familiar and found in your pantry. In the event you find yourself out of an ingredient or haven't yet included a particular ingredient as your norm, the following substitution list may be helpful.

SWEETENERS

1 cup **molasses** = ¾ cup **dark brown sugar** + ¼ cup **water**

1 cup **brown sugar** = 1 cup **sugar** + 2 Tbsp **molasses**

FATS

1 cup **margarine** = 1 cup **butter** = ⅞ cup **oil**

1 cup **heavy cream** = 1 cup **nondairy whipping cream** = 1 cup **nondairy creamer**

ACIDS

1 cup **buttermilk** = 1 Tbsp **lemon juice** *or* **white vinegar** + enough **milk** *or* **pareve milk** to make 1 cup

1 Tbsp **red wine vinegar** = 3 Tbsp **apple cider vinegar** + 1 Tbsp **red wine** *or* 1 Tbsp **white wine vinegar**

1 Tbsp **apple cider vinegar** = 1 Tbsp **red wine vinegar** *or* 1 Tbsp **white wine vinegar**

1 Tbsp **white wine vinegar** = 1 Tbsp **red wine vinegar**

1 Tbsp **balsamic vinegar** = 1 Tbsp **apple cider vinegar** *or* **red wine vinegar** + ½ tsp **sugar**

1 Tbsp **sherry vinegar** = 1 Tbsp **apple cider vinegar** + splash **sherry wine**

1 Tbsp **rice vinegar** = 1 Tbsp **apple cider vinegar**

1 tsp **lime juice** = 1 tsp **lemon juice** = 1 tsp **vinegar** *or* 1 tsp **dry white wine**

HERBS AND FLAVORINGS

1 tsp **hot sauce** = ¾ tsp **cayenne pepper** + 1 **tsp vinegar**

1 tsp **miso paste** = ½ tsp **ketchup** + ½ tsp **soy sauce**

1 **vanilla bean** = 1 Tbsp **vanilla extract**

1 tsp **basil** = 1 tsp **thyme** = 1 tsp **oregano** = 1 tsp **sage**

1 tsp **cumin** = 1 tsp **coriander**

1 tsp **cardamom** = ½ tsp **nutmeg** *or* **ginger** + ½ tsp **cinnamon**

1 tsp **cayenne pepper** = 1 tsp **hot paprika**

1 tsp **liquid smoke** = 1 tsp **smoked paprika**

VEGETABLES

2 cups fresh **chopped tomatoes** = 1 (14.5 oz) can **diced tomatoes**

1 tsp **onion** = 1 tsp **chives** = 1 tsp **leek** = 1 tsp **scallion**

shallot = **Vidalia onion**

MISCELLANEOUS

Lotus cookies = **graham crackers** = **gingersnaps**

Starters

PULLED BEEF NACHOS WITH PEACH SALSA

Meat   YIELDS *8-12 servings*

Dressed up or dressed down, these nachos will definitely be the most popular dish at your party.

Sweet and Sour Brisket

1 (3-5-lb)	second cut brisket
•	kosher salt, to taste
•	black pepper, to taste
6 cloves	garlic, crushed
½ cup	ketchup
½ cup	chili sauce
2 Tbsp	sweet chili sauce
½ cup	grape jelly
½ cup	light beer

Peach Salsa

½ cup	fresh parsley leaves
2	ripe peaches *or* nectarines, diced
½	red bell pepper, finely diced
3	scallions, thinly sliced
2	avocados, finely diced
1 Tbsp	olive oil
1 Tbsp	white wine vinegar
1 Tbsp	lime juice
1 Tbsp	lemon juice
1 tsp	hot sauce, such as Frank's
•	kosher salt, to taste

Tortilla Nacho Chips

¼ cup	olive oil
1 tsp	kosher salt
1 clove	garlic, crushed
1 package	(6-inch) round tortilla wraps

1. **Prepare the sweet and sour brisket:** Preheat oven to 325°F. Prepare a 9x13-inch baking pan.

2. Rinse brisket; pat dry. Place into prepared baking pan. Season brisket with salt and pepper. Smear crushed garlic over meat.

3. Combine ketchup, chili sauces, and grape jelly; whisk until smooth. Pour over meat. Pour beer around brisket. Cover with foil.

4. Bake 2½-3 hours, or until fork tender. Transfer meat to a large dish; shred meat with 2 forks.

5. **Prepare the peach salsa:** Finely mince parsley leaves. In a medium bowl, toss together parsley, fruits, and vegetables. In a second bowl, whisk together olive oil, vinegar, lime juice, lemon juice, and hot sauce. Add dressing to fruit/vegetable mixture. Sprinkle with salt. Allow to sit for 30 minutes for flavors to blend.

6. **Prepare the tortilla nacho chips:** Preheat oven to 350°F. Line a baking sheet with parchment paper.

7. In a small bowl, combine olive oil, salt, and garlic. Place 3 wraps on prepared baking sheet. Smear each wrap with olive oil mixture. Cut each tortilla into 8 wedges. (A pizza cutter works well here).

8. Bake for 10 minutes. Remove from oven; transfer to a platter. Repeat until all wraps are baked into chips (see Note).

9. To serve, place a mound of pulled brisket onto the center of a serving platter. Set nacho chips on the platter; top with peach salsa or set salsa alongside meat.

—Note

If making chips in advance, store in a baking pan or on a platter, uncovered overnight. In the morning, transfer to a resealable bag or airtight container.

MEATBALLS AND ZOODLES

Meat   YIELDS *10 servings*

Zoodles are a healthy and aesthetically appealing alternative to traditional pasta. This fun appetizer will be enjoyed by young and old alike.

1 lb	ground beef
1	egg
½ cup	seasoned panko crumbs
½ tsp	garlic powder
1 tsp	onion powder
1 tsp	ground mustard
3 Tbsp	nondairy milk

BBQ Sauce

¼ cup	ketchup
2 Tbsp	water
1 Tbsp	apple cider vinegar
1 Tbsp	dark brown sugar, packed
1 Tbsp	honey
1 tsp	onion powder
¼ tsp	ground mustard
½ tsp	lemon juice
½ tsp	balsamic vinegar

Zoodles

7½ cups	zucchini zoodles (approximately 5 zucchinis)
3 Tbsp	olive oil
1 Tbsp	kosher salt
½ tsp	black pepper

Special Equipment

10	bamboo or metal skewers (soak bamboo skewers in water for ½ hour before using)

1. Preheat oven to 400°F. Line 2 baking sheets with parchment paper.

2. In a large bowl, combine ground beef, egg, panko crumbs, spices, and nondairy milk. Mix well until ingredients are completely incorporated. Form into 20 golf-ball-size balls; set aside.

3. **Prepare the BBQ sauce:** In a small saucepan, stir together all sauce ingredients. Bring to a boil (or microwave for 2 minutes in a microwave-safe bowl). Remove from heat.

4. Thread 2 meatballs onto a small skewer; place on 1 prepared baking sheet. Repeat with remaining meatballs.

5. Brush each meatball with BBQ sauce. Bake, uncovered, for 10 minutes.

6. Remove from oven. Turn over each skewer. Brush with BBQ sauce. Bake, uncovered, for 10-15 minutes.

7. **Prepare the zoodles:** Spread zoodles on remaining baking sheet. Toss with olive oil, salt, and pepper until well coated.

8. Roast, uncovered, for 10 minutes, tossing once after 5 minutes. Remove from oven.

9. To serve, plate 1 skewer over ¾ cup zoodles.

— Note —————————————————

These meatballs freeze beautifully.

STUFFED BABY BELLA MUSHROOMS

Meat

YIELDS *24 stuffed mushrooms*

Stuffed mushrooms make an easy and delicious appetizer (or snack!) for any party or special get-together. The savory pastrami breadcrumb stuffing takes these mushrooms to the next level.

24	baby bella mushrooms
¼ cup	fresh parsley leaves
2 Tbsp	olive oil
1 small	shallot, finely diced
4 oz	pastrami, diced finely (approximately 6 slices)
2 cloves	garlic, crushed
¼ cup	seasoned breadcrumbs
2 Tbsp	teriyaki sauce

1. Preheat oven to 350°F. Line a baking sheet with parchment paper; lightly coat with cooking spray.

2. **Prepare the stuffing:** Remove mushroom stems; finely dice stems. Finely mince parsley; set aside.

3. In a medium frying pan, heat olive oil over medium-high heat. Add shallot and diced stems; sauté for 3 minutes. Add pastrami and crushed garlic. Cook 1 minute.

4. Remove pan from heat; stir in breadcrumbs and minced parsley.

5. Fill mushroom caps with the stuffing; Place, stem-side up, on prepared baking sheet. Drizzle with teriyaki sauce.

6. Bake, uncovered, for 20 minutes, or until mushrooms are tender.

SHREDDED BBQ CHICKEN BITES

Meat   YIELDS *8 servings*

My friend's daughter, Yaeli, came back from vacation and told me about an incredible appetizer that she had eaten while dining out, and she asked me to replicate it and include it here. This definitely lives up to its reputation.

Rice Patties

3 cups   cooked rice (cooked in broth), cooled

3 Tbsp   flour

1   egg

•   oil, for frying

Shredded BBQ Chicken

3 cups   chicken broth

2 lb   boneless chicken cutlets

1 cup   BBQ sauce (page 202), *or* any BBQ sauce

3 Tbsp   oil

•   sea salt, to taste

•   black pepper, to taste

•   Balsamic Reduction (page 130)

Peanut Sauce

⅓ cup   peanut butter

⅓ cup   coconut milk

1 Tbsp   canola oil

1 Tbsp   rice vinegar

½ Tbsp   teriyaki sauce

1 tsp   sriracha

1 clove   garlic, crushed

1.   **Prepare the rice patties:** Prepare a baking sheet.

2.   Combine cooked rice, flour, and egg; allow mixture to sit 10 minutes. With greased hands, form rice patties, using ⅓ cup rice per patty. Place patties on prepared baking sheet; freeze for 30 minutes.

3.   Heat oil in a skillet over medium heat. Fry patties 3-4 minutes per side, until lightly golden. Set aside.

4.   **Prepare the shredded BBQ chicken:** In a large pot, over high heat, bring chicken broth to a boil. Add chicken; lower heat to a medium-low simmer. Cover; cook, stirring occasionally, until chicken can be easily shredded, about 25 minutes. Transfer chicken to a bowl; set aside. Reserve ½ cup chicken broth; refrigerate or freeze remainder for another purpose. Using tongs, squeeze chicken until shredded. Return chicken, BBQ sauce, reserved broth, and oil to the pot. Cook mixture over medium heat until liquid is absorbed, about 5 minutes. Season with salt and pepper.

5.   **Prepare the peanut sauce:** Using a whisk, combine all sauce ingredients.

6.   **To serve:** Place a rice patty in the center of each plate. Divide shredded chicken between the patties. Drizzle with peanut sauce and balsamic reduction (see Note).

— Tip —

It's a good idea to prepare the rice the day before and refrigerate overnight.

If you are making chicken soup, place chicken cutlets into a mesh bag and cook in boiling soup for 25 minutes; then continue with recipe.

— Note —

To easily drizzle the peanut sauce and balsamic reduction, pour each into a squeeze bottle or place in a resealable bag and snip the corner.

MOROCCAN LAMB CHILI

Meat   YIELDS *8 servings*

Quick and easy, this hearty chili is packed with flavor. It is very versatile and I often use it as a crowd-pleasing main.

2 Tbsp	olive oil
1 medium	onion, diced
1 lb	ground lamb
4 cloves	garlic, crushed
⅛ tsp	red pepper flakes, or more to taste
1 tsp	dried basil
1 tsp	coriander
3½ Tbsp	chili powder
1	bay leaf
1 tsp	sea salt
pinch	black pepper
1 (14½-oz) can	garlic and basil-flavored diced tomatoes with their liquid
2 (15½-oz) can	chickpeas, rinsed and drained
2 Tbsp	lemon juice

1. In a large stock pot or Dutch oven, over medium-high heat, heat oil. Add onion; sauté until soft, about 5 minutes. Push onion to the side of the pan. Add lamb, stirring and breaking apart large lumps as it browns and cooks through, for 5 minutes. Add garlic, pepper flakes, basil, coriander, chili powder, bay leaf, salt, and pepper. Cook for 1 minute.

2. Carefully pour in tomatoes with their liquid; stir in chickpeas. Bring mixture to a boil; reduce heat. Simmer, scraping up any brown bits on the bottom of the pot, until liquid reduces, about 15 minutes. Stir in lemon juice; adjust salt and pepper if necessary.

3. Remove and discard bay leaf before serving.

Variation

Ground beef can be substituted for the ground lamb.

DUCK CONFIT CROSTINI WITH L'ORANGE GLAZE

Meat   YIELDS 16 servings

With my trusty l'orange glaze, the resulting duck is exceedingly tender, moist, and extremely flavorful. Although the process may seem long, the actual hands-on time is not.

Duck Confit

3 Tbsp	kosher salt, plus more to taste
¼ tsp	black pepper, plus more to taste
4 cloves	garlic, crushed
½ tsp	dried thyme *or* **4** fresh sprigs thyme
1	bay leaf, crumbled
4	duck legs

L'Orange Glaze

2 Tbsp	honey
¼ cup	orange juice
½ Tbsp	low sodium soy sauce
½ Tbsp	lemon juice
½ Tbsp	duck sauce
½ Tbsp	apricot jam
•	sea salt, to taste
•	black pepper, to taste

Crostini

1	long baguette, sliced into 16 (½-inch) slices
2 Tbsp	olive oil
•	kosher salt, to taste
•	black pepper, to taste
•	scallions *or* chives, for garnish
•	strips of orange zest, for garnish

1. **Prepare the duck confit:** In a small bowl, combine salt, pepper, garlic, thyme, and bay leaf. Season duck generously with mixture. Place in a pan or skillet in one layer. If using fresh thyme, spread sprigs over duck. Cover tightly with plastic wrap; refrigerate overnight, up to 24 hours.

2. Preheat oven to 325°F.

3. In an ovenproof skillet, place duck legs, skin-side down, fitting snugly in a single layer. Over medium-high heat, cook until fat begins to render. After 15 minutes, when there is about ⅛-inch fat rendered, turn legs over. Cover skillet; place in oven. Roast for 1½ hours.

4. Remove from oven; uncover skillet. Return to oven and continue roasting until duck is golden brown, about 1 hour. Remove duck from fat (you may reserve fat for other uses); transfer to a cutting board. Remove duck skin; set aside. Remove meat from bones; discard bones. Slice meat into thin strips.

5. Season duck skins with salt and pepper. Sear in a medium skillet over medium heat, pressing down on the skins to make contact with the pan. Turn occasionally until skins are golden brown and crisp, about 6 minutes. Transfer skins to a paper towel to drain. Cool; crumble into small pieces.

6. **Prepare the l'orange glaze:** in a small saucepan, over medium heat, heat glaze ingredients. When heated through, pour half the sauce over duck strips; toss to coat. Season with salt and pepper.

7. **Prepare the crostini:** Preheat oven to 425°F. Prepare a baking sheet.

8. Arrange 16 baguette slices on prepared baking sheet. Drizzle with olive oil; season with salt and pepper. Bake until golden, 6-8 minutes. Set aside.

9. **To assemble:** Spoon duck mixture onto crostini. Top with sliced scallions, duck skin cracklings, a drizzle of l'orange glaze, and strips of orange zest.

GLAZED SWEETBREADS

Meat YIELDS *6-8 servings*

A delicacy that my family eagerly looks forward to enjoying, these sweetbreads truly enhance our Yom Tov meals.

2 lb	veal sweetbreads
1 Tbsp	vinegar
3 Tbsp	olive oil
1	onion, diced
4 oz	baby bella mushrooms, sliced
•	sea salt, to taste
•	black pepper, to taste
2 Tbsp	red wine vinegar
1 Tbsp	silan

1. Place sweetbreads into a medium saucepan with water to cover; add vinegar. Bring to a boil over medium-high heat. Low boil for 30 minutes. Rinse under cold water for 5 minutes. Remove sweetbreads from protective membrane. Set aside.

2. In a large skillet, heat olive oil over medium heat. Add onion; sauté for 10 minutes. Add mushrooms. Season with salt and pepper; sauté until soft, 5 minutes. Add sweetbreads, red wine vinegar, and silan; cook for 1 minute. Lower heat; simmer until tender, about 20 minutes. Adjust seasoning to taste.

3. Serve warm in individual bowls. Alternatively, serve family style as a wonderful main course.

— Note

If you do not have silan, substitute honey. The taste will differ slightly.

SKEWERED SEA BASS WITH SWEET 'N SOUR DIPPING SAUCE

Pareve YIELDS *8 servings*

Skewering the cubes allows this melt-in-your-mouth delicacy to become an affordable classic at your table. Paired with this versatile sauce with only 5 ingredients and 5 minutes of prep time, this delicious dish couldn't be simpler!

1 lb	sea bass, cut into 24 (1-inch) cubes
⅓ cup	duck sauce
½ cup	seasoned panko crumbs

Sweet 'N Sour Dipping Sauce

¼ cup	light brown sugar, packed
1 Tbsp	lime juice
1 Tbsp	unseasoned rice vinegar
¼ cup	chili sauce
¼ cup	sweet chili sauce
•	greens, for serving, optional

Special equipment

8	bamboo or metal skewers (soak bamboo skewers in water for ½ hour before using)

1. Preheat oven to 400°F. Line a baking sheet with parchment paper.

2. **Prepare the sea bass:** Place duck sauce into one bowl and panko crumbs in a second bowl. Dip each fish cube into duck sauce, turning to coat. Dip each coated cube into panko crumbs, turning to coat. Place coated cubes on prepared baking sheet; bake for 15 minutes. Remove from oven; allow to cool.

3. **Prepare the sweet 'n sour dipping sauce:** Place brown sugar into a small bowl. Pour lime juice and vinegar over sugar; stir until sugar has completely dissolved. Add both chili sauces; stir until completely blended.

4. **To serve:** Thread 3 sea bass cubes onto each skewer. If desired, place skewers onto a bed of greens. Drizzle fish with dipping sauce, or serve with additional sauce.

SALMON AND KANI CEVICHE

Pareve   YIELDS *6-8 servings*

Light and packed with flavor, this ceviche is really over the top.

1 lb   sushi grade salmon, diced finely

½ cup   fresh parsley leaves

1   scallion, finely diced

½ lb   kani, defrosted and diced

1   jalapeño pepper, seeded and finely diced

•   watermelon radish, sliced, for garnish

Citrus Dressing

6 Tbsp   lime juice

2 Tbsp   orange juice

1 Tbsp   ketchup

1 tsp   prepared white horseradish

½ tsp   sriracha

¼-½ tsp   sea salt

⅛ tsp   black pepper

1. **Prepare the citrus dressing:** In a small bowl, whisk together dressing ingredients. Refrigerate until cold.

2. Finely mince parsley leaves. In a large bowl, toss together salmon, parsley, scallion, kani, and jalapeño pepper. Pour dressing over salmon/kani mixture. Toss to coat.

3. Garnish with watermelon radish slices for a healthy, crunchy "cracker."

— Note

Ceviche (seh-vee-chay) is made by curing fresh raw fish in citrus juices and spicing with seasonings.

MUSHROOM RAVIOLI

Dairy   YIELDS *16 ravioli*

This classic Italian dish with its robust flavors is sure to wow everyone at your table. To make it nondairy, sub in margarine, nondairy cream cheese, and nondairy milk.

3 Tbsp	butter or olive oil
¼ cup	onion, finely chopped
1½ cups	baby bella mushrooms, finely chopped
2 oz	block-style cream cheese
¼ tsp	sea salt
⅛ tsp	black pepper
32	ravioli dough rounds *or* round wonton wrappers

White Sauce

2 Tbsp	flour
1 Tbsp	canola oil
1 cup	half-and-half or heavy cream
6 oz	block-style cream cheese
1-2 cloves	garlic, crushed
⅛ tsp	nutmeg
½ tsp	white pepper

1. In a medium frying pan, melt butter over medium heat; add onion and sauté for 3 minutes. Lower heat, add mushrooms, and cook 3 minutes. Stir in cream cheese, salt, and pepper; remove from heat.

2. Fill a 6-quart pot halfway with water; bring to a rolling boil. While the water is coming to a boil, place a small spoonful of mushroom mixture onto the center of a ravioli dough round. Moisten the entire rim of the dough with water; cover with a second round, making sure to line up the two rounds perfectly. Use your fingers to seal the ravioli by pressing the edges down very well. Repeat until all the ravioli are prepared.

3. Drop 4-5 ravioli into boiling water. Don't cook too many at once or they will stick to each other. When the ravioli are cooked through (5-7 minutes), they will float to the top. Remove with a slotted spoon; place on paper towels to drain. Repeat with remaining ravioli.

4. **Prepare the white sauce:** In a small saucepan, over low heat, whisk flour and oil until a roux forms (see Note). Add half-and-half; cook over medium-low heat, constantly stirring, until slightly thickened, about 3 minutes. Bubbles will begin to form around the edges, but don't bring to a rolling boil or it may burn. As soon as it begins to thicken and the bubbles form, add cream cheese; stir until completely melted and incorporated. Stir in garlic, nutmeg, and white pepper. Remove from heat.

5. To serve, place 1-2 ravioli onto center of a small plate. Spoon warmed white sauce over ravioli; serve immediately.

— Note —

To make a roux, whisk together oil and flour, over low heat, until the flour is completely incorporated and the mixture becomes pasty. Mixture may look slightly lumpy at first; continue whisking until smooth.

Brunch, Lunch, & Beyond

BLUEBERRY PANCAKES WITH BLUEBERRY SYRUP

Dairy YIELDS *20 pancakes*

These pancakes are so tasty I even love them without the sauce! You can enjoy these pancakes any time of year, using fresh or frozen blueberries.

2 cups	flour
5 tsp	baking powder
¼ cup	sugar
1 Tbsp	vanilla sugar
½ tsp	sea salt
2	eggs
1¾ cups	milk
1 cup	sour cream
2 Tbsp	canola oil
1 cup	fresh *or* frozen blueberries

Blueberry Syrup

2 cups	fresh blueberries
½ cup	sugar
1 cup	water, divided
1 tsp	vanilla extract
2 Tbsp	lemon juice
1 Tbsp	cornstarch

1. **Prepare the blueberry syrup:** In a small saucepan over medium heat, combine blueberries, sugar, and ½ cup water. Cook until berries begin to pop. Stir in vanilla extract and lemon juice.

2. In a cup or bowl, combine cornstarch with remaining ½ cup water; stir until cornstarch has dissolved. Add to blueberry mixture. Stir until mixture thickens slightly; mixture will cloud initially and then become glossy.

3. **Prepare the pancakes:** In a large mixing bowl, combine flour, baking powder, sugars, and salt. In a second bowl, use a fork or whisk to lightly beat the eggs; beat in milk, sour cream, and oil. Stir milk mixture into dry ingredients until moistened. Fold blueberries into batter.

4. Heat a frying pan or griddle. Lightly grease frying pan. Pour ¼ cup batter into the pan. Flip over when bubbles begin to form on top. Fry until golden. Set aside. Repeat until all batter is used.

5. Serve warm pancakes with blueberry syrup. Store any remaining blueberry syrup in the refrigerator.

—Tip—

Blueberries can be tossed with 2 tablespoons flour to keep the juices from running.

BUTTER CROISSANTS

Dairy **YIELDS** *16 croissants*

Most croissant recipes are very tedious and time-consuming. This recipe, however, uses a technique that results in soft, buttery goodness without all the fuss.

4½ tsp dry yeast
(2 [½-oz] packets)

¾ cup warm water (110-115°F)

½ cup sugar, divided

1 tsp kosher salt

2 eggs

½ cup butter, softened
(1 stick)

4 cups flour

4 Tbsp butter, melted
(½ stick)

1. Line a baking sheet with parchment paper.

2. Pour warm water into a bowl. Add yeast and 2 tablespoons sugar. Stir to dissolve the yeast. Proof until yeast doubles in volume, about 10 minutes.

3. Add remaining sugar, salt, eggs, ½ cup butter, and flour; mix together by hand. Let dough rise at least 30 minutes.

4. Divide the dough in half; form into balls. Roll one ball into a 10-inch circle. Brush with melted butter. Use a pizza cutter to cut the circle into 8 segments. Roll each segment from the wider end to the narrow end to form croissants. Repeat with remaining dough.

5. Lay each croissant on prepared baking sheet with the tip underneath. Let rise for 30 minutes.

6. Preheat oven to 375°F.

7. Bake for 15 minutes, or until slightly golden. Let cool slightly before serving.

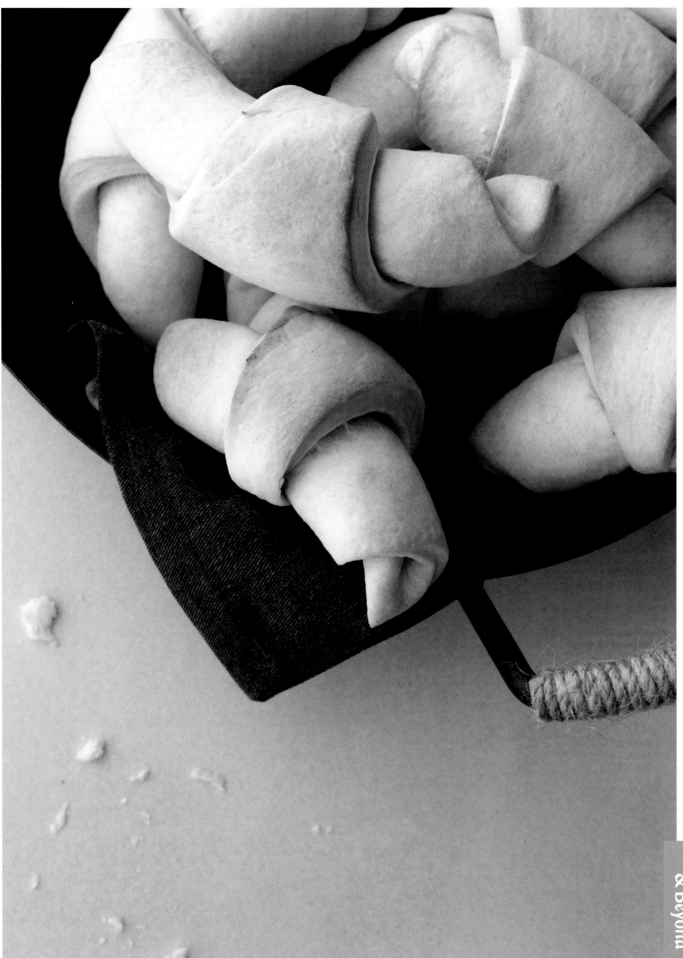

SUNNY-SIDE-UP BOATS

Dairy   YIELDS *8 servings*

Nothing beats a relaxing, lazy, Sunday. While enjoying your family time, everyone will also be enjoying these easy, breezy, sunny-side-up boats.

8   pretzel rolls *or* any hard bread rolls

1 small   onion, diced finely

•   kosher salt, to taste

•   black pepper, to taste

4 tsp   butter

8   eggs

8 tsp   Parmesan cheese, for sprinkling

1. Preheat oven to 350°F. Line a baking sheet with parchment paper.

2. Cut a thin slice off the top of each roll. Carefully remove the center of each roll, leaving a ½-inch shell. (You can use the bread you remove for a stuffing or to make croutons.) Place sandwich boats onto the prepared baking sheet.

3. Place 1 teaspoon diced onion inside a boat cavity; sprinkle with salt and pepper. Place ½ teaspoon butter into the center. Carefully crack an egg; pour it over the onion (without breaking the yolk). Sprinkle with additional salt and pepper and 1 teaspoon Parmesan cheese. Repeat with remaining boats.

4. Bake for 15-17 minutes, until the egg whites are set and the yolks are still runny.

5. Serve immediately.

CARROT MUFFINS WITH MAPLE-CHEESE FROSTING

Dairy YIELDS *12 muffins*

Moist and delicious, these carrot muffins topped with creamy frosting are always a winner.

Muffin

1 cup	all-purpose flour
1 cup	whole wheat flour
2 tsp	baking soda
2 tsp	cinnamon
¼ tsp	nutmeg, optional
¼ tsp	sea salt
2 cups	shredded carrots (from about 2 large carrots)
3	eggs
1 cup	canola oil
2 tsp	vanilla extract
1 cup	dark brown sugar
1	Granny Smith apple, peeled and shredded

Maple-Cheese Frosting

8 oz	cream cheese, at room temperature
1 cup	powdered sugar
1 tsp	pure maple syrup

1. Preheat oven to 350°F. Grease or line with paper liners 1 (12-cup) cupcake pan.

2. In a large bowl, sift together flours, baking soda, cinnamon, nutmeg, and salt. Stir in shredded carrots.

3. In a medium bowl, whisk together eggs, oil, vanilla, and sugar. Stir in shredded apple.

4. Pour egg/apple mixture over the flour/carrot mixture; stir until well combined.

5. Fill cupcake cups ¾ full.

6. Bake for 20 minutes. Test with a toothpick; it should come out clean. Allow to cool.

7. **Prepare the maple-cheese frosting:** Whip cream cheese until smooth. Add powdered sugar and maple syrup. Beat until completely incorporated.

8. Spread or pipe frosting over cooled muffins.

BREAKFAST MUFFINS

Pareve   YIELDS *12 muffins*

You may find it hard to believe that muffins that taste this good are actually good for you! Bake, freeze, and grab one for a quick breakfast or snack on the go.

1	egg
¼ cup	canola oil
¾ cup	unsweetened applesauce
1 tsp	baking powder
1 tsp	baking soda
½ cup	honey
1 tsp	vanilla extract
1 cup	old-fashioned oats
1 cup	whole wheat flour
¾ tsp	cinnamon
1 cup	mini chocolate chips

1. Preheat oven to 350°F. Line 1 (12-cup) cupcake pan with paper liners.

2. In a medium bowl, whisk together egg and oil. Add applesauce; whisk until smooth. Add remaining ingredients; stir until incorporated.

3. Fill cupcake cups ¾ full.

4. Bake 18-20 minutes, until slightly golden and a toothpick inserted into the center comes out clean.

MAPLE PECAN GRANOLA

Pareve YIELDS *6 servings*

1 cup	old-fashioned oats
½ cup	coconut flakes (large chips)
½ cup	chopped pecans
¼ cup	turbinado sugar
¼ cup	dark brown sugar, packed
2 Tbsp	pure maple syrup
2 Tbsp	canola oil

Homemade granola is so much tastier than store bought, and it's so easy to make. While shooting pictures for this cookbook, everyone kept munching on the photo-ready jar of granola. We all joked that this should be called "Disappearing Granola"!

1. Preheat oven to 350°F. Line a stainless steel baking sheet with parchment paper or coat with cooking spray.

2. Combine all ingredients on prepared baking sheet. Toss gently to evenly coat. Spread into a single layer.

3. Bake for 15 minutes, stirring once halfway through baking.

4. Remove from oven; cool.

5. Store in a resealable bag or airtight container.

Tip

A stainless steel baking sheet is recommended because it gets hotter and heats more evenly than a disposable pan. This will yield a very crunchy granola.

Note

Turbinado sugar is a light brown cane sugar similar to demerara sugar, with larger crystal.

PITAYA BOWL

Dairy

YIELDS *1 large bowl or 2 small bowls*

1 cup fresh *or* frozen pitaya (dragon fruit) cubes

1 cup frozen tropical fruit cubes (strawberry, mango, pineapple)

¼ cup strawberry Greek yogurt

¼ cup milk

¼ cup apple, orange, or fruit juice of your choice

Assorted Toppings

- granola, homemade (see page 44) or store-bought
- cocoa nibs
- coconut chips
- blueberries
- banana slices
- mango cubes
- almond butter

Dragon fruit is a magnificent and exotic-looking fruit. Paired with tropical fruits and yogurt, it makes an incredibly colorful and healthy meal.

1. Place pitaya, frozen fruit, yogurt, milk, and juice into a blender. Blend until completely smooth.

2. Transfer to a bowl. Top with toppings of your choice. Serve immediately.

MALAWAH CALZONES

Dairy YIELDS *6 servings*

Classic vegetable-and-cheese calzone wrapped in flaky, crispy, heavenly goodness.

Filling

2 Tbsp	butter or olive oil
1 small	red onion, finely diced
½	orange pepper, finely diced
4 oz	white mushrooms, sliced *or* **1 (8-oz) can** sliced mushrooms, drained
½ cup	frozen chopped spinach, defrosted and squeezed dry
1 clove	garlic, crushed
1	scallion, sliced
1 tsp	sea salt, plus more, to taste, divided
½ tsp	black pepper, plus more, to taste, divided
½ cup	shredded cheese (Muenster, mozzarella, or Mexican blend)
¼ cup	cottage cheese
2 Tbsp	cream cheese *or* sour cream
½ tsp	garlic powder

1 package	malawah dough (6 rounds), defrosted
3 Tbsp	duck sauce, for brushing
•	sesame seeds, for garnish, optional

1. **Prepare the filling:** Heat butter in a medium skillet over medium-high heat. Add onion; sauté for 3 minutes, until softened. Add remaining vegetables. Season with 1 teaspoon sea salt and ½ teaspoon black pepper. Sauté for 7 minutes, stirring occasionally.

2. Add shredded cheese; stir until cheese begins to melt. Add cottage cheese and cream cheese; stir until cheese mixture is completely smooth. Season with additional salt and pepper to taste; add garlic powder. Stir to combine. Remove pan from heat. Cool slightly.

3. **Prepare the calzones:** Preheat oven to 400°F. Line a baking sheet with parchment paper.

4. Place 1 malawah dough round on your workspace. Place 2-3 tablespoons of filling onto the center of the round. Fold dough in half; seal by pressing edges together. Reinforce the seal by pressing down around edges with a fork. Transfer calzone to prepared baking sheet. Repeat with remaining malawah rounds and filling.

5. Brush each calzone with duck sauce. Garnish with sesame seeds, if desired.

6. Bake on center rack for 20-25 minutes, until golden. Serve hot.

FULLY LOADED VEGGIE BURGERS

Pareve   YIELDS *6 servings*

This quick and easy burger is packed with flavor. It makes a great, healthy, budget-friendly family meal.

1 (15-oz) can	black beans, rinsed, 6 Tbsp liquid reserved
1 (15-oz) can	chickpeas, rinsed and drained
2 Tbsp	flour
4	scallions, minced
3 Tbsp	fresh parsley leaves
2 cloves	garlic, crushed
1 tsp	coriander
1 tsp	sriracha
½ tsp	chili powder
¼ tsp	sea salt
¼ tsp	black pepper
½ cup	crushed enchilada tortilla chips *or* barbecue corn chips
¼ cup	canola oil, divided
6	pitas, for serving
•	lettuce, for serving
•	tomato slices, for serving
•	Roasted Garlic Aoili Sauce, (page 166)

1. Set aside reserved 6 tablespoons liquid from can of black beans. Line a baking sheet with 3 layers of paper towels. Spread chickpeas and beans over the towels and allow to rest 15 minutes.

2. In a large bowl, whisk together reserved bean liquid and flour until combined and smooth. Finely chop parsley. Add scallions, chopped parsley, garlic, coriander, sriracha, chili powder, salt, and pepper. Mix until well combined.

3. Process enchilada chips in a food processor until finely ground. Add beans; pulse until smooth. Transfer bean mixture into flour mixture; mix until combined.

4. Divide mixture into 6 portions; form into 3½-inch well-packed patties. Optional but recommended: Refrigerate patties for ½ hour to firm.

5. In a large skillet over medium heat, heat 1 tablespoon oil. Gently place 3 patties into skillet; cook until well crisped and browned, about 5 minutes. Flip over; cook until browned, 3-5 minutes.

6. Preheat oven to 200°F.

7. Toast pitas in oven for 2-3 minutes. Serve each burger in a pita with Roasted Garlic Aioli Sauce, lettuce, and tomato slices.

CREAMY MUSHROOM PASTA

Dairy YIELDS *6-8 servings*

This truly is a restaurant-worthy dairy delicacy.

8 oz	fettucine
2 Tbsp	butter
1 lb	sliced steak mushrooms or large baby bella mushrooms
2 cloves	garlic, crushed
1 tsp	pareve beef broth powder, dissolved in ⅓ **cup** water
⅓ cup	semisweet or dry white wine
1½ tsp	low sodium soy sauce
1 tsp	cornstarch
2 tsp	Dijon mustard
1 tsp	sea salt
¼-½ tsp	black pepper
½ cup	heavy cream
1 Tbsp	dried parsley flakes

1. Prepare pasta according to package instructions. Drain; rinse and set aside.

2. Melt butter in a large skillet over medium-high heat. Add sliced mushrooms and garlic. Stir until well coated. Sauté for 10-15 minutes until all mushrooms are slightly browned. Transfer to a bowl.

3. Combine pareve beef broth, wine, soy sauce, cornstarch, mustard, salt, and pepper in a small bowl. Add mixture to the skillet; bring to a boil. Stir until mixture begins to thicken, about 1 minute. Add cooked pasta and mushrooms; stir to coat.

4. Add heavy cream and parsley flakes. Stir until well combined.

5. Remove from heat and serve.

RAVIOLI WITH VELVETY SPINACH SAUCE

Dairy YIELDS *6 servings*

I absolutely love ravioli. With the fast-paced lifestyles that we all lead, I appreciate the convenience of pre-made pastas. Paired with a simple fish and salad, these ravioli complete a marvelous meal.

2 (9-oz) packages frozen cheese ravioli *or* spinach and cheese ravioli

Velvety Spinach Sauce

½ cup (1 stick) butter

1 onion, diced

3 cloves garlic, crushed

1½ cups frozen chopped spinach, thawed and squeezed dry

2 cups (1 pint) heavy cream

8 oz sour cream

¼ cup Parmesan cheese

1 tsp sea salt

½ tsp black pepper

1. Prepare ravioli according to package directions. Remove from boiling water with a slotted spoon; drain on paper towels.

2. **Prepare the velvety spinach sauce:** In a medium pot over medium heat, melt butter. Add onion and garlic; sauté until translucent, about 7 minutes. Add spinach; sauté 2 minutes. Add heavy cream and sour cream. Stir until completely incorporated. Stir in Parmesan cheese, salt, and pepper. Simmer 5 minutes.

3. Transfer ravioli from paper towels to a serving dish. Pour spinach sauce over the ravioli. Toss to completely coat. Serve warm.

ONION AND MUSHROOM CREPE PIE

Dairy   YIELDS *8-10 servings*

I was developing this recipe when the East Coast of the United States was hit with Hurricane Sandy, one of the most destructive natural disasters on record. Out of power, but not out of ideas, I created this stovetop crepe pie.

Crepe Batter

3	eggs
¾ cup	flour
pinch	sea salt
1 Tbsp	sugar
1 cup	milk

Onion-Mushroom Cream Sauce

2 Tbsp	olive oil
1 small	red onion, diced
8 oz	baby bella mushrooms, sliced
1 pint (2 cups)	heavy cream
3 Tbsp	flour
2 cloves	garlic, crushed
1 tsp	sea salt
½ tsp	black pepper
⅓ cup	grated Parmesan cheese

1. **Prepare the crepes:** Combine all crepe ingredients in a large mixing bowl. Place paper towels on your counter or work surface. Coat a 6-inch frying pan with cooking spray; heat over medium-high flame. Pour ¼-cup batter into heated pan. Tilt pan to spread batter evenly. When crepe looks dry, turn; fry for a few seconds. Transfer crepe to a prepared paper towel (lay each crepe separately; do not overlap crepes). Set aside. You should have 6-8 crepes.

2. **Prepare the onion-mushroom cream sauce:** Heat olive oil in a medium frying pan. Add onion; sauté for 3 minutes. Add sliced mushrooms; sauté an additional 3 minutes. Add heavy cream; sprinkle with flour; stir to combine. Add remaining sauce ingredients. Bring to a boil; stir until thickened and smooth.

3. **Assemble the pie:** Place 1 crepe onto a large round plate. Spread 2 heaping tablespoons onion-mushroom mixture over crepe. Top with a second crepe and onion-mushroom mixture. Continue alternating crepes and onion-mushroom mixture, ending with onion-mushroom mixture.

4. Cut into wedges to serve; serve warm.

CRUSTLESS ONION AND CHIVE QUICHE

Dairy   YIELDS *8 servings*

Quiche is perfect for breakfast, lunch, or dinner and is so easy to make. This quiche is crustless, light, and scrumptious. Feel free to improvise and add in any vegetables of your choice.

2 Tbsp	butter
3 large	sweet onions, sliced
1	leek (white and light green parts only), diced
½ cup	chives, cut into 1-inch pieces
2 cups	shredded cheddar cheese
¾ cup	half and half
4	eggs
½ tsp	sea salt
¼ tsp	black pepper

1. Preheat oven to 350°F. Prepare an oven-to-table baking dish or a 9x13-inch baking pan.

2. In a large frying pan over medium-high heat, melt butter. Add onions and leek; sauté, stirring often, 15-20 minutes, until mixture becomes caramel colored. Remove from heat. Add 2 tablespoons chives and cheese. Stir to combine. Cool slightly.

3. In a medium bowl, whisk together half and half, eggs, salt, and pepper. Pour mixture into the onion/chive mixture; mix well. Pour mixture into prepared baking dish. Sprinkle with remaining chives.

4. Bake 40-45 minutes, until set. Cool 15 minutes before serving.

SPINACH AND CHEESE CRISPY-SKIN BAKED POTATOES

Dairy   YIELDS *4 servings*

Perfectly crisped skins and fabulously flavored filling elevate the humble potato.

4	baking potatoes, scrubbed and dried
1 Tbsp + **¼ cup**	olive oil, divided
1 small	onion, finely chopped
2 cups	frozen chopped spinach, defrosted and squeezed dry to make ½ cup
2 cloves	garlic, crushed
½ cup	cottage cheese
¾ tsp	garlic powder
½ tsp	sea salt
¼ tsp **+ ½ tsp**	black pepper, divided
¾ tsp	kosher salt
8 tsp	shredded Parmesan cheese, optional

1. Preheat oven to 425°F.

2. Use a fork to pierce potatoes all over. Bake potatoes directly on the center rack of oven for 1 hour. If necessary, bake up to 15 additional minutes to ensure potatoes are fully baked.

3. In a small saucepan, heat 1 tablespoon olive oil; add onion. Cook over medium heat for 5 minutes. Stir occasionally until onions are softened but not browned. Set aside.

4. Slice potatoes in half lengthwise. Scoop out the flesh, leaving a ¼-inch shell, and placing potato flesh into a bowl. Add spinach, onion/oil mixture, cottage cheese, garlic powder, salt, and ¼ teaspoon pepper. Mix well.

5. Turn oven to broil. Line a baking sheet with parchment paper.

6. Combine remaining ¼ cup olive oil, kosher salt, and ½ teaspoon pepper in a small cup. Brush potato skins and inside of each potato with the olive oil mixture. Lay potatoes skin-side up on prepared baking sheet.

7. Broil potatoes for 3 minutes. Turn potatoes flesh-side up; broil 3 additional minutes.

8. Lower oven temperature to 425°F.

9. Fill crispy potato skins with potato/spinach mixture; return to oven. Bake for 20 minutes.

10. **Optional:** Sprinkle each potato half with 1 teaspoon Parmesan cheese. Bake 5 additional minutes.

11. Serve immediately.

SEASONAL FRUIT SALAD

Pareve   YIELDS *8 servings*

Get creative and change the fruits with the changing seasons. One thing is for sure, this dressing will work all year round.

1 cup   mango, diced

1 (8-oz) can   mandarin oranges (whole segments), drained

1 cup   strawberries, halved

1 cup   blueberries

1 cup   black cherries, halved and pitted

1   kiwi, peeled, sliced, and quartered

½ cup   red grapes, halved

•   grilled peach slices, optional

Dressing

6 Tbsp   canola oil

3 Tbsp   lime juice *or* orange juice

3 Tbsp   honey

¼ tsp   vinegar

¾ tsp   fresh grated ginger *or* ½ **cube** frozen ginger or ¼ **tsp** ground ginger

1. Combine dressing ingredients.

2. Layer salad ingredients or toss together.

3. Drizzle with dressing.

LIMONANA

Pareve   YIELDS *10 servings*

I often host parties and get-togethers in my home. None are complete without this simply refreshing, always requested drink.

1 (12-oz) can frozen lemonade concentrate

5 cups water

1 pint lemon sorbet

2 lemons, sliced

• mint leaves, optional

1 cup ice cubes *or* crushed ice

1. Pour lemonade concentrate into a 1-gallon pitcher. Add water and sorbet. Add sliced lemon and mint leaves. Stir well.

2. Add ice. Serve cold.

BUTTER PECAN MILKSHAKES

Dairy YIELDS *2 milkshakes*

Nothing beats a rich, creamy milkshake. With a bit of crunch, caramel, and chocolate, this is the ideal sweet treat.

2½ cups	butter pecan ice cream
½ cup	milk
3 sticks	white Viennese Crunch, crushed
¼ cup	caramel cream
½ Tbsp	vanilla sugar

Optional Toppings

- whipped cream
- caramel cream
- chocolate syrup
- Viennese Crunch crumbs

1. In a blender or with an immersion blender, mix ice cream, milk, Viennese Crunch, caramel cream, and vanilla sugar.

2. **Prepare 2 large glasses:** Drizzle caramel cream down the inside of each glass. Divide ice cream mixture between glasses. Garnish with toppings of choice.

Salads

DIPPING TRIO

Pareve   YIELDS *vary*

Whether you make these delicious dips for your Shabbos table or as accompaniments at your family BBQ, you'll find that they are all very versatile and always a hit.

WASABI MAYO

½-1 **tsp**	wasabi powder
½ **tsp**	honey
1½ **tsp**	lemon juice
½ **cup**	mayonnaise

1. In a small bowl, combine wasabi powder, honey, and lemon juice; whisk until the powder has dissolved.

2. Add mayonnaise; stir until the mixture is smooth.

ONION MARMALADE

1 (6.5-oz) **package**	frozen sautéed onions (10 squares; see Note)
3 **Tbsp**	dark brown sugar
½ **tsp**	kosher salt
•	black pepper, to taste
2 **Tbsp**	red wine vinegar

1. In a small saucepan, over medium heat, add onion cubes; stir to begin defrosting. Add brown sugar. Add salt and pepper. Stir until onions are completely defrosted.

2. Add red wine vinegar; simmer for 10 minutes. Allow mixture to cool before serving.

— Note —

To caramelize fresh onions, heat 1 tablespoon oil in a saucepan; add a small diced onion, ½ teaspoon salt, and black pepper, to taste. Sauté for 12-15 minutes, over low heat, until onion is translucent. Add 3 tablespoons dark brown sugar. Raise heat, stirring constantly, until onion has caramelized. Continue with Step 2 above.

BBQ MAYO

» In a measuring cup or small bowl, stir together all ingredients until completely combined.

½ **cup**	mayonnaise
2 **Tbsp**	barbecue sauce
2 **Tbsp**	sweet chili sauce
1 **tsp**	sriracha
¼ **tsp**	yellow mustard

ROASTED PEPPER TAPENADE

Pareve   YIELDS *1½ cups*

¼ cup	olive oil
3	red bell peppers, diced
4	jalapeño peppers, sliced, seeded, and diced
1 head	garlic, separated into cloves, peeled
2 Tbsp	dried parsley flakes
1 tsp	sea salt

I was always afraid that a recipe with jalapeños would taste too hot. My friend Penina asked me to try her produce manager's recipe for jalapeño dip. Tried it, tweaked it, and now make it every Shabbos. Never say never.

1. In a sauté pan over medium heat, heat olive oil. Add peppers and garlic; sauté until soft (15-20 minutes), stirring occasionally.

2. Turn off heat. Add parsley and salt. Transfer to a tall (rather than wide) container; puree with an immersion blender.

3. Refrigerate. Tapenade will stay fresh in an airtight container in the fridge for up to 2 weeks.

ROASTED OLIVES

Pareve   YIELDS *10-12 servings*

2 (19-oz) cans pitted green olives, drained

5-6 canned hot peppers (see Note)

1 head garlic, separated into cloves, peeled

3 Tbsp olive oil

The first time I tasted these outstanding olives was in Israel, at the home of Chani S. Their flavor packs a punch and they are so simple to prepare. These olives have become a Shabbos staple in my home, and in the homes of my friends and family.

1. Preheat oven to 350°F. Prepare a baking sheet.

2. Spread olives, hot peppers, and garlic cloves on baking sheet in a single layer. Drizzle with olive oil. Toss to coat well.

3. Bake for 60-75 minutes; stirring occasionally.

4. Serve at room temperature. Store in an airtight container in the refrigerator; olives will stay fresh for 2-3 weeks.

— Note —

Transfer remaining canned peppers to a container; refrigerate until ready to use.

WALDORF SLAW

Pareve   YIELDS *10 servings*

This crispy slaw delivers satisfaction with every crunchy bite.

1 (14-oz) bag	shredded cabbage
1½ cups	shredded red cabbage
2	Granny Smith apples, with peel, cored and cut into matchsticks
2 ribs	celery, diced
½ cup	fresh blueberries
½ cup	red onion, diced
½ cup	whole cashews

Dressing

½ cup	apple cider vinegar
⅓ cup	sugar
⅓ cup	canola oil
½ tsp	sea salt
¼ tsp	black pepper
¼ tsp	onion powder
¼ tsp	garlic powder

1. In a large serving bowl, toss together cabbages, apples, celery, blueberries, red onion, and cashews.

2. **Prepare the dressing:** In a small saucepan, over medium heat, bring vinegar, sugar, and oil to a boil. Stir in salt and spices. Set aside to cool slightly.

3. Pour dressing over salad; toss to coat well.

—Tip—

This salad gets better as it absorbs the dressing, so it's perfect to prepare in advance.

GRILLED VEGETABLE AND KALE SALAD

Pareve   YIELDS *12 servings*

My family always looks forward to a good barbecue. With that in mind, I figured that adding these marinated grilled vegetables to a salad would be a great idea ... and it sure was!

Marinade

¼ cup	olive oil
2 Tbsp	lemon juice, preferably fresh
4 cloves	garlic, crushed
¼ tsp	kosher salt
¼ tsp	black pepper

Salad

3	Portobello mushrooms, gills removed
1	red bell pepper, cut into 8 pieces
1	yellow bell pepper, cut into 8 pieces
1	orange pepper, seeded, cut into 8 pieces
1	yellow squash, sliced into ¼-inch oval discs
1	green zucchini, sliced into ¼-inch oval discs
1 small	red onion, cut into wedges
16-oz	kale or mixed greens, shredded

Dressing

¼ cup	extra light olive oil
¼ cup	vinegar
¼ cup	honey
1¼ Tbsp	low sodium soy sauce
2 cloves	garlic, crushed

1. Combine marinade ingredients in a large resealable bag. Add mushrooms, peppers, squash, zucchini, and onion. Toss to coat; marinate for 30 minutes.

2. Preheat grill. Grill mushrooms, peppers, squash, and zucchinis for 4 minutes each side. Grill onion wedges for 6 minutes on each side. Alternatively, broil on high for 10 minutes on 1 side and additional 5 minutes on second side.

3. After grilling, slice mushrooms into ½-inch-thick slices.

4. **Prepare the dressing:** In a small bowl, whisk together all dressing ingredients until smooth.

5. **Assemble the salad:** Place kale into a large serving bowl; top with grilled vegetables. Drizzle with dressing; toss to coat.

GARDEN SALAD WITH BREADED MUSHROOMS

Pareve   YIELDS *12 servings*

While preparing a family simchah, I was on the hunt for a new, interesting salad. Deena Weiss, the Salad Queen, was kind enough to share this winner. If fewer servings are needed, simply use half of all the ingredients and continue with the recipe.

2 (9-oz) bags romaine lettuce *or* spring mix

2 pints grape tomatoes, halved

1 red onion, sliced

1 cup slivered almonds, toasted

1 cup onion-and-garlic-flavored croutons

Breaded Mushrooms

1 (10-oz) box baby bella or button mushrooms (smaller mushrooms work best here)

3 eggs

1 cup flour

½ tsp sea salt

¼ tsp black pepper

1 cup cornflake crumbs

Dressing

1 cup mayonnaise

1 Tbsp yellow mustard

2-3 cloves garlic, crushed

3 Tbsp lemon juice

1 Tbsp sugar

¾ tsp sea salt

½ tsp black pepper

1. Preheat oven to 450°F. Line a baking sheet with parchment paper; coat well with cooking spray.

2. **Prepare the breaded mushrooms:** Rinse mushrooms; pat dry.

3. Prepare a breading station with 3 bowls. Whisk eggs in one bowl; set aside. Mix flour and spices in the second bowl; set aside. Pour cornflake crumbs into the third bowl.

4. Dredge mushrooms in flour, dip in eggs, then coat completely with cornflake crumbs.

5. Place breaded mushrooms on prepared baking sheet without crowding them. Coat very well with cooking spray. Bake 15 minutes until golden, turning once. Remove from oven; allow to cool. See Note.

6. **Prepare the dressing:** In a small bowl or container, combine dressing ingredients.

7. **Assemble the salad:** In a large bowl, combine all salad ingredients. Dress and toss the salad right before serving.

— Tip —

Mushrooms may be breaded in advance and frozen before baking. Defrost, uncovered, before baking. Alternatively, you can make your life easier and buy frozen breaded mushrooms. Store-bought or homemade mushrooms can be fried or baked in a jiffy.

BROCCOLI ROMAINE SALAD WITH CRANBERRY VINAIGRETTE

Pareve   YIELDS *6 servings*

You know how some salads just work? This salad is an all-around favorite but particularly a favorite of my daughter-in-law, Shana. It will surely become one of yours, too.

¼ cup	pine nuts, toasted
¼ cup	chopped pecans, toasted
1 (8-oz) bag	romaine lettuce
1 (8-oz) package	fresh broccoli florets (see Note)
⅓ cup	dried cranberries
1 bunch	scallions, cleaned and thinly sliced

Dressing

¼ cup	jellied cranberry sauce
2 Tbsp	mayonnaise
1½ Tbsp	red wine vinegar
2 tsp	Dijon mustard

1. **Toast the nuts:** Preheat oven to 350°F. Arrange nuts in a single layer in a baking pan. Place in heated oven for 5 minutes. Remove from oven; allow to cool.

2. In a small bowl, whisk together all dressing ingredients until smooth.

3. In a large serving bowl, combine all salad components. Pour dressing over salad; toss before serving.

— Note —————————

If fresh broccoli is not available, you may substitute frozen broccoli. Place broccoli into a strainer or colander and run under hot water, drain well, and then proceed as directed above.

HEIRLOOM TOMATO SALAD

Pareve   YIELDS *8 servings*

This fresh, simple salad is best made with vine-ripened heirloom tomatoes, but toss in any type of tomatoes you have on hand, because the dressing is simply sensational.

2 pints	heirloom grape tomatoes, sliced
1 bunch	scallions, sliced
¼ cup	fresh parsley, finely chopped, optional

Dressing

¼ cup	olive oil
1 Tbsp	fish-free Worcestershire sauce
2 cloves	garlic
1 tsp	lemon juice
3 Tbsp	mayonnaise
3 Tbsp	sugar
1 tsp	ground mustard
1 Tbsp	dried parsley flakes

1. Place all dressing ingredients into a blender; mix well. Alternatively, place ingredients into a tall container and blend with an immersion blender.

2. In a large serving bowl, toss salad ingredients with dressing to coat.

TERIYAKI MUSHROOM SALAD

Pareve   YIELDS *8-10 servings*

Colorful, fresh, and eye-catching as well, this visually appealing salad is as tasty as it is beautiful.

1 (4-oz) bag baby spinach leaves

1 (8-oz) bag shredded red cabbage

1 bunch scallions, sliced

½ orange pepper, sliced into 1-inch matchsticks

½ yellow pepper, sliced into 1-inch matchsticks

1 cup grape tomatoes, halved

Teriyaki Mushrooms

1 Tbsp olive oil

8-10 oz baby bella mushrooms, washed and quartered

½ tsp kosher salt

¼ tsp black pepper

1 Tbsp teriyaki sauce

Dressing

3 Tbsp mayonnaise

¼ cup white wine vinegar

¼ cup honey

3 cloves garlic, crushed

Topping

1 oz sweet chili-flavored *or* barbeque PopCorners *or* corn chips

3 Tbsp toasted sesame seeds (see Note)

1. **Prepare the teriyaki mushrooms:** In a 2-quart saucepan over medium heat, heat olive oil. Add quartered mushrooms, salt, and pepper. Sauté for 5 minutes, covered. Add teriyaki sauce; stir. Raise heat to high; cook until all liquid is absorbed, about 1 minute. Remove from heat; allow to cool.

2. **Prepare the dressing:** In a small bowl or container, whisk together dressing ingredients.

3. **Assemble the salad:** In a large bowl, toss together all salad ingredients. Add dressing; toss to coat. Top with PopCorners and teriyaki mushrooms; sprinkle with toasted sesame seeds.

— Note

To toast sesame seeds, place seeds into a small baking pan. Preheat oven to 350°F; toast seeds in preheated oven for 5-7 minutes.

PERFECT PASTA SALAD

Pareve or Dairy

YIELDS *6 servings*

1 (1-lb) box gemelli pasta or pasta of your choice

⅓ cup olive oil

1 Tbsp freshly squeezed lemon juice

1 clove garlic, crushed

1 tsp kosher salt

½ tsp dried basil

½ tsp dried oregano

¼ tsp black pepper

½ cup shredded Parmesan cheese, divided, optional

A wonderful, light, and savory pasta salad that can be served anytime, anywhere.

1. Cook pasta according to package instructions. Drain; return to pot.

2. In a small bowl, combine oil, lemon juice, garlic, and spices; pour over pasta. If using, sprinkle most of the Parmesan cheese over the pasta. Stir over medium heat for 1 minute.

3. Transfer to a serving bowl; sprinkle with remaining Parmesan cheese, if using. Serve warm or at room temperature.

Variation

Change up this salad by adding in any fresh or roasted vegetables.

SWEET POTATO FETA SALAD

Dairy   YIELDS *6 servings*

Delicious and vibrant with bright colors, this salad is truly extraordinary. While I love the peppery flavor of arugula, you can definitely substitute with romaine.

3	medium sweet potatoes, thinly sliced
3 Tbsp	olive oil
1 Tbsp	kosher salt
¼ tsp	black pepper
1 (8-oz) package	chopped arugula *or romaine*
1	avocado, diced
1 cup	fresh spiralized beets
1 cup	golden berries (gooseberries), halved
½ cup	grated feta cheese
½ cup	toasted pine nuts
¼ cup	fresh parsley, chopped

Red Wine Vinaigrette

⅓ cup	olive oil
⅓ cup	red wine vinegar
3 Tbsp	honey
½ tsp	sea salt
¼ tsp	black pepper

1. Preheat oven to 400°F. Line a baking sheet with parchment paper; coat lightly with cooking spray.

2. Place sweet potato slices in a single layer on prepared baking sheet. Drizzle with olive oil. Season with salt and pepper; toss well. Bake for 40 minutes, tossing once. Remove from oven; cool.

3. **Prepare the red wine vinaigrette:** In a small saucepan, over medium heat, bring olive oil and red wine vinegar to a boil. Simmer for 3 minutes. Remove from heat. Stir in honey. Season with salt and pepper; let cool.

4. In a large serving bowl, toss together salad ingredients. Whisk dressing well; drizzle onto salad. Toss well before serving.

— Note —

Spiralized beets can be purchased in many grocery stores or prepared at home using a spiralizer or julienne peeler.

CAFE-STYLE GREEK SALAD

Dairy YIELDS *6 servings*

1 (8-oz) bag	shredded romaine lettuce
1	red onion, thinly sliced
1 cup	black pitted olives, drained
2	plum tomatoes, cut into wedges, *or* grape tomatoes, halved
1	cucumber, peeled, seeded, and sliced
½ cup	feta cheese, crumbled

Dressing

½ cup	mayonnaise
2 Tbsp	balsamic vinegar
2 heaping Tbsp	powdered sugar

While fashions change and trends come and go, there are a few tried-and-true classics that have withstood the test of time. Greek salad definitely qualifies as one of those. This creamy balsamic dressing really adds wonderful depth to this culinary classic.

1. In a large bowl, toss together all salad ingredients.

2. **Prepare the dressing:** In a small bowl, whisk together dressing ingredients.

3. Pour dressing over salad; toss to coat well.

CHIMICHURRI HANGER STEAK SALAD

Meat YIELDS *6-8 servings*

The marinated, tender hanger steaks make this savory salad a meat lover's dream.

2	hanger steaks
8 oz	arugula
1	ripe avocado, sliced
1 cup	grape tomatoes, halved
handful	pine nuts, toasted, optional

Marinade

4 Tbsp	olive oil
4 Tbsp	red wine vinegar
2 Tbsp	lemon juice
2 cloves	garlic, crushed
1 tsp	kosher salt
1 tsp	chili powder
1 tsp	dried oregano

Chimichurri Sauce

1¼ cup	flat leaf parsley, leaves only
¼ cup	olive oil
¼ cup	red wine vinegar
4 cloves	garlic, crushed
1	jalapeño pepper, seeded and chopped
1 tsp	dried oregano
1 tsp	sea salt

1. **Prepare the chimichurri sauce:** In the bowl of a food processor fitted with the "S" blade or in a deep bowl, combine all sauce ingredients. Pulse in the food processor or with an immersion blender until combined; you will still see small pieces. Allow to rest for at least 1 hour to allow flavors to blend.

2. Submerge hanger steak in cold water for 20 minutes to soak away the meat's saltiness.

3. Combine marinade ingredients in a large resealable bag. Add steaks; marinate for 20 minutes.

4. Broil or sear meat for 4-5 minutes per side. If preparing in advance, store steaks in refrigerator until ready to serve. Discard remaining marinade.

5. **To serve:** Slice steak against the grain into ½-inch slices. Place a small handful of arugula in the center of each plate. Add avocado, tomatoes, and pine nuts, if using. Top salad with steak slices. Dress with chimichurri sauce.

RETRO DELI SALAD

Meat   YIELDS *8 servings*

My inspiration for this salad was good old deli and mustard. It is versatile, easy, and downright delicious. I serve it at Shabbos meals, weekday dinners, and even at barbecues. The continuously empty bowl is all the proof that I need that this recipe just always works.

1 (8-oz) bag romaine lettuce

⅓ lb dried hard salami, thinly sliced *or* beef jerky, sliced

1 red onion, thinly sliced

1 avocado, cubed

1 cup barbeque corn nuts (or any spicy flavor)

1 cup grape tomatoes, halved

Dressing

½ cup extra light olive oil

¼ cup apple cider vinegar

¼ cup honey

½ Tbsp yellow mustard

1 clove garlic, crushed

1 tsp sea salt

¼ tsp black pepper

1. In a small bowl or container, combine all dressing ingredients.

2. In a large serving bowl, layer salad ingredients. Pour dressing over salad; toss well.

PORTOBELLO AND CHICKEN SALAD

Meat   YIELDS *6 servings*

The combination of meaty Portobellos, tender chicken, crisp cabbage, and maple mustard dressing will appeal to all flavor profiles.

6	Portobello mushroom caps, gills removed, sliced
4	chicken cutlets
1 (8-oz) bag	romaine lettuce
1 (8-oz) bag	shredded red cabbage
1 cup	bean sprouts
1 cup	grape tomatoes, halved

Marinade

½ cup	olive oil
4 Tbsp	low sodium soy sauce
3 Tbsp	stone ground mustard
1 Tbsp	pure maple syrup, optional
2 Tbsp	lemon juice
1 tsp	black pepper
1 tsp	garlic powder

Dressing

¼ cup	olive oil
¼ cup	pure maple syrup
2 Tbsp	apple cider vinegar
2 Tbsp	lemon juice
½ tsp	kosher salt
¼ tsp	black pepper

1. In a large bowl, combine all marinade ingredients. Divide evenly between 2 resealable bags. Place chicken into one bag and sliced mushrooms into the other bag. Marinate for at least 30 minutes (can be marinated overnight).

2. Preheat oven to 400°F. Set out 2 (9x13-inch) pans, one for the chicken and one for the mushrooms.

3. Transfer chicken and mushrooms separately into prepared pans. Bake, uncovered, for 30 minutes. Alternatively, chicken may be grilled. Cut chicken into ½-inch strips.

4. **Prepare the dressing:** In a small bowl, whisk together all dressing ingredients.

5. **To serve:** In a large serving bowl, layer romaine, red cabbage, bean sprouts, and grape tomatoes. Top with chicken strips and mushrooms. Drizzle with dressing.

SAUSAGE SALAD

Always on the lookout for new and different ideas, I decided to find out how sausage would work in a salad. You can choose mild or spicy sausage, play with the flavors, and customize it to your taste preference. Whichever you choose ... enjoy!

1 Tbsp	olive oil
1	onion, sliced
1 (7-oz) package	sausage, sliced
2 Tbsp	dark brown sugar
1 Tbsp	teriyaki sauce
1 Tbsp	ketchup
1 (8-oz) bag	shredded romaine lettuce
1 cup	everything bagel rounds *or* pretzel thins

Dressing

3 Tbsp	olive oil
1 Tbsp	lemon juice
1 tsp	Dijon mustard
1 Tbsp	honey
1 clove	garlic, crushed
½ tsp	sea salt
¼ tsp	black pepper

1. Heat a medium frying pan over medium heat; add oil. Sauté onion in hot oil until golden, about 10 minutes. Raise heat; add sausage slices. Stir 1 minute; add brown sugar, teriyaki sauce, and ketchup. Stir until combined; remove from heat. (This can be prepared in advance and refrigerated.)

2. **Prepare the dressing:** In a small bowl, whisk together dressing ingredients.

3. **To serve:** In a large bowl, toss together lettuce and meat mixture with pan juices. Add dressing; toss to coat well. Top with bagel rounds.

Soups

BUTTERNUT SQUASH SOUP WITH FRENCH TOAST CROUTONS

Pareve YIELDS *8 servings*

Savory and satisfying, this soup is an all-new butternut squash experience. With the surprising addition of the crouton sweetness and the optional crunchy squash seeds, these flavor combinations can't be beat.

Roasted Vegetables

1 small	head garlic
1 Tbsp	canola oil
•	kosher salt
•	black pepper
2 lb	fresh butternut squash, cubed, seeds reserved
5 large	shallots, sliced
1 medium	onion, sliced

Soup

⅓ cup	canola oil
1 Tbsp	kosher salt
½ tsp	black pepper
6 cups	vegetable broth, *or* **6 cups** water + **2 Tbsp** vegetable soup mix
2 Tbsp	kosher salt
½ tsp	black pepper

French Toast Croutons

3½-4 cups	1-inch bread cubes
¼ cup	sugar
2 Tbsp	canola oil
1 Tbsp	nondairy milk
1 tsp	cinnamon

Crunchy Seed Topping

2 Tbsp	olive oil
½ cup	butternut squash seeds, rinsed and dried
½ tsp	kosher salt
½ tsp	garlic powder
¼ tsp	black pepper

1. **Prepare the roasted vegetables:** Preheat oven to 400°F. Line a baking sheet with parchment paper.

2. Slice off the top of the garlic head, so that the tips of the garlic cloves are visible. Place the garlic head onto a piece of foil large enough to enclose garlic. Drizzle with oil. Sprinkle with salt and pepper. Seal foil; place garlic on prepared baking sheet.

3. Add butternut squash, shallots, and onion to the baking sheet. Drizzle with oil. Sprinkle with salt and pepper. Toss vegetables until well coated. Roast, uncovered, for 1 hour.

4. **Prepare the French toast croutons:** Preheat oven to 400°F. Line a baking sheet with parchment paper; coat with cooking spray

5. In a large bowl, whisk together sugar, oil, milk, and cinnamon. Add bread cubes; toss to coat. Transfer bread cubes to prepared baking sheet in 1 layer.

6. Bake for 10 minutes.

7. **Prepare the crunchy seed topping:** Slightly heat a small frying pan over medium heat. Dip a pastry brush into olive oil; brush the bottom of the skillet until well coated.

8. Pour butternut squash seeds into the skillet. Stir seeds continuously until they puff slightly and begin to brown. Transfer seeds to a bowl; toss with salt, garlic powder, and pepper

9. **Prepare the roasted butternut squash soup:** Squeeze roasted garlic cloves out of their peels into a 6-quart pot. Add roasted vegetables. Add vegetable broth, salt, and pepper.

10. Stir well; bring mixture to a boil. Lower heat; simmer for 40 minutes.

11. Use an immersion blender to puree soup right in the pot. Serve with croutons and/or crunchy seed topping.

EXOTIC WILD MUSHROOM SOUP

Pareve   **YIELDS** *10 servings*

¼ **cup**	olive oil
2	onions, diced
4 cloves	garlic, crushed
3 Tbsp	kosher salt, divided
½ **tsp**	black pepper, divided
20 oz	wild mushrooms, sliced (see Note)
1 oz	dried porcini mushrooms
10 cups	water
¼ **tsp**	nutmeg
¼ **cup**	sherry cooking wine
¼ **cup**	fresh dill (leaves only), measured and finely chopped
¾ **cup**	wild rice

Almost everyone has either cooked with or eaten fresh mushrooms. The intense flavor that is achieved by adding dried mushrooms is absolutely delightful. The result is a rich, satisfying soup that is an all-new experience.

1. Heat olive oil in an 8-quart pot over medium-low heat. Add onions, garlic, 1 tablespoon salt, and a pinch of pepper. Sauté for about 20 minutes, stirring occasionally. Raise heat to high; stir constantly for 3-5 minutes as the mixture caramelizes and begins to become golden.

2. Add wild mushrooms; sauté for 5 minutes. Add remaining salt and pepper; add remaining ingredients and bring to a rolling boil. Lower heat to a simmer; cook for 45 minutes, stirring occasionally.

3. This soup will thicken when refrigerated. You may add water when reheating. Adjust salt and pepper to taste.

— Note ———————————

Many grocery stores sell packages of wild mushrooms, which include shitake, oyster, and cremini mushrooms. If unavailable, buy an assortment of these mushrooms.

MINESTRONE SOUP WITH GNOCCHI CROUTONS

Pareve   **YIELDS 10-12 servings**

I absolutely love a hearty soup and minestrone is one of my favorites. This recipe is quick and healthy. With the addition of the gnocchi, it is a perfect filling meal all in one bowl. This is sure to become one of your favorites, too.

4 Tbsp	olive oil
2	red onions, diced
4	leek, diced (white and light green part only)
8 ribs	celery, diced
3 Tbsp	kosher salt, divided
4 large	zucchini, with peel, diced
4 large	sweet potatoes, peeled and diced
8 cloves	garlic, crushed
2 (15-oz) cans	chickpeas, rinsed and drained
12 cups	water
1 Tbsp	consommé powder, optional
4 tsp	paprika
2 tsp	turmeric
2	bay leaves
½ tsp	black pepper
¼ tsp	cayenne pepper
2 (14-oz) cans	diced tomatoes with their liquid
1 tsp	ground ginger
1 (16-oz) package	nondairy gnocchi

1. In a 10- or 12-quart pot, heat olive oil over a medium heat; add onions, leek, and celery with 1 tablespoon salt. Sauté for 5 minutes. Stir; add all remaining ingredients except the gnocchi.

2. Bring soup to a boil, then lower heat and simmer for 45 minutes.

3. Remove from heat. Add gnocchi. Allow to rest for 5-10 minutes before serving.

SIMPLY PERFECT SPLIT PEA SOUP

Pareve   **YIELDS** *8 servings*

Looking for a quick and versatile pareve soup to add to (or start?) any meal? Try this thick and satisfying soup with fabulous flavor that's ready in less than an hour.

4 Tbsp	olive oil
2 medium	onions, diced
4 cloves	garlic, crushed
2 cups (16-oz bag)	green split peas, rinsed
8 cups	water
1 Tbsp	kosher salt
½-¾ tsp	black pepper
2 tsp	hot sauce, such as Frank's

1. In a 6-quart pot, heat olive oil over a medium heat; add onions and garlic. Sauté for 10 minutes.

2. Add remaining ingredients. Bring to a boil. Lower heat to a simmer; cook for 45-60 minutes, or until split peas are tender. Stir occasionally so the peas don't stick to the bottom of the pot.

ANNIE'S LOW-CAL SUMMER FRUIT SOUP

Pareve   YIELDS *12 servings*

When I think of sweet summer memories, my first thought is of my dear friend Annie Neuman a"h. Annie was a balabusta par excellence. With her sudden passing, my summers will truly never be the same. I am honored to share Annie's recipe for this perfect summer soup.

12 cups	water
1 (28-oz) can	fruit cocktail with its juice
1 (15-oz) can	diced peaches with its juice
2-3	plums, diced
2	firm Bartlett or Anjou pears, diced
12 oz	frozen strawberries, sliced in half
1 (16-oz) box	blueberries
15	cherries, pitted and halved
1	lemon, sliced into rings
1	lime, sliced into rings, optional
¼ tsp	sea salt

1. In an 8-10 quart pot, bring water to a boil.

2. Add fruit cocktail and peaches with their juices. Add plums and pears. Bring to a boil over medium heat; boil for 5-7 minutes.

3. Add strawberries, blueberries, and cherries. Cook for 30 minutes, stirring occasionally.

4. Add lemon and lime rings; add salt. Cook for 15 minutes.

5. Turn off heat; place hot pot in a sink full of ice cold water. Change water frequently to cool.

6. After 15 minutes, remove lemon and lime slices. Reserve for garnish. Soup will have a beautiful purple color.

7. Serve cold, garnished with reserved lemon and lime slices.

CHESTNUT APPLE SOUP

Pareve **YIELDS** *8-10 servings*

My friend Goldie mentioned that her daughter Rachel, a nutritionist, makes a fabulous chestnut apple soup. Curious, I played with the idea and made my own version. I agree! This healthful soup is actually amazing!

2 Tbsp	margarine
2 Tbsp	olive oil
2 cups	shallots, coarsely chopped
1 cup	celery, chopped (about 4 ribs)
1 tsp	sea salt, divided
½ tsp	black pepper, divided, plus more, to taste
4 cups	Pink Lady apples, peeled and diced (about 4 apples)
1 tsp	dried thyme
3 cups	vegetable broth (*or* **3 cups water +** **1½ Tbsp** vegetable broth powder)
3 cups (20-oz)	whole, peeled, roasted chestnuts
1 cup	almond milk
2 cups	water
•	sea salt, to taste

1. Melt margarine in a large pot over medium heat. Add olive oil, shallots, and celery. Sauté, stirring continuously, for 5 minutes. Season with ½ teaspoon salt and ¼ teaspoon pepper.

2. Add apples and thyme. Season with additional ½ teaspoon salt and ¼ teaspoon pepper. Cook, stirring occasionally, for 10 minutes until apples are tender.

3. Add broth, chestnuts, almond milk, and water. Bring to a boil. Reduce heat; simmer until apples and celery are tender, about 15 minutes.

4. Use an immersion blender to puree soup in the pot. Season with sea salt and pepper to taste.

CHEESY CREAMY BROCCOLI SOUP

Dairy YIELDS *8 servings*

Nothing is more satisfying than coming up with a winner in a pinch. My inspiration for this soup came toward the end of a long fast day. I needed to create something quickly that would feed lots of hungry people. Everyone gave this soup two thumbs up.

6 Tbsp	garlic butter, divided (see Note)
1 large	onion, diced
2 Tbsp	kosher salt, divided
24 oz	fresh or frozen broccoli
4 cloves	garlic, crushed
6½ cups	vegetable stock *or* **6½ cups water + 2 Tbsp** consommé powder
1 tsp	garlic powder
⅛ tsp	nutmeg
½ tsp	black pepper
3 Tbsp	flour
1 cup	Mexican Blend shredded cheese, packed
2 oz	Pepper Jack cheese
¼ cup	grated Parmesan cheese
1 cup	heavy cream

1. Melt 3 tablespoons garlic butter in an 8-quart pot over medium-high heat. Add onion and 1 teaspoon salt; sauté for 2 minutes. Add broccoli; cook for 6 minutes. Add garlic; cook for 1 minute. Add stock, remaining salt, and spices; bring to boil. Simmer, uncovered, for 15 minutes, or until broccoli is tender.

2. Use an immersion blender to puree soup in the pot.

3. Melt remaining 3 tablespoons garlic butter in the microwave. In a small bowl, mix the melted butter with flour to form a paste. Whisk paste into the soup. Add in all cheeses; simmer until soup thickens, stirring frequently.

4. Once soup is thickened and all cheeses have melted, add heavy cream; warm through. Do not bring to a boil, as boiling may cause cream to curdle.

— Note

To make your own garlic butter, mix together 6 tablespoons softened butter and 1 cube/clove crushed garlic.

LAMB AND BARLEY SOUP

Meat   YIELDS *10 servings*

There's nothing like a steaming bowl of soup on a cold winter day. This hearty soup is a delicious, filling meal all in one bowl.

3 lb	lamb stew meat or lamb breast meat, bone in
4	carrots, diced, divided
4 ribs	celery, diced, divided
1	daikon radish, diced
3	zucchini, peeled and diced, divided
1	spice bouquet of ¼ **cup** fresh parsley and ¼ **cup** fresh dill
12 cups	water
3-4 Tbsp	kosher salt, divided
½-¾ tsp	chili powder
2 Tbsp	olive oil
1 large	onion, diced
2 small	leeks, diced (white and light green part only)
½ cup	barley
½-¾ tsp	black pepper

1. Place meat into an 8-10-quart pot. Add half the carrots, celery, daikon, and zucchini. Add the spice bouquet. Add water with 1 tablespoon kosher salt and chili powder. Bring to a boil; lower heat. Simmer for 1½ hours.

2. Meanwhile, heat olive oil in a sauté pan over medium heat. Add onion and leek; sauté for 20 minutes, or until translucent. Raise heat; stir continuously until onions caramelize. Remove from heat; set aside.

3. Remove meat from pot. Cool slightly. Remove and discard bones. Remove and discard spice bouquet.

4. Skim fat from the soup. If preparing in advance, refrigerate for 3-5 hours or overnight, until a slight layer of fat forms; lift off and discard the fat. If refrigerating soup at this point, refrigerate the meat and onion mixture in separate containers.

5. After skimming the fat, place the pot on the stove. Return meat to the pot. Add barley, remaining vegetables, and caramelized onion mixture. Bring to a boil over medium-high heat. Cook for 30 minutes, or until barley and vegetables are tender. Season with remaining 2-3 tablespoons salt and pepper. Serve hot.

Note

A spice bouquet is made by placing fresh aromatics (herbs) into a fine mesh bag or a tied cheese cloth. This allows the flavor of the aromatics to be infused into the soup and provides easy disposal.

A daikon radish is a mild-flavored Chinese radish that resembles a thick, smooth, white carrot.

CAULIFLOWER SOUP
WITH BEEF-FRY CROUTONS

Meat   YIELDS 8 servings

This is one of my all-time favorites, a creamy soup that's flavorful and filling. The crisped beef fry adds an amazing taste and texture that make this the ultimate comfort food.

1 (24-oz) bag	frozen cauliflower, defrosted and drained
3 Tbsp	olive oil
2 Tbsp	kosher salt, divided
1 tsp	black pepper, divided
4 oz	beef fry (about 6 slices)
4 ribs	celery, sliced
1 small	onion, diced
2 cloves	garlic, crushed
3 Tbsp	fresh dill leaves
⅓ cup	sherry wine
6 cups	chicken broth *or* **6 cups water + 2 Tbsp** chicken soup mix
¾ cup	almond milk *or* any nondairy milk
2	bay leaves

1. Preheat oven to 400°F. Line a baking sheet with parchment paper.

2. Toss cauliflower with oil, 1 tablespoon kosher salt, and ½ teaspoon pepper. Spread on prepared baking sheet. Roast until golden brown, 35-40 minutes.

3. Slice beef fry width-wise into very short, narrow strips. Place into a 6-quart pot over medium-high heat. Cook, stirring occasionally, until browned and crisp, 10-12 minutes (it will pop and splatter within the pot). Remove crisped beef fry with a slotted spoon; drain on paper towels and set aside. Do not discard rendered fat.

4. Add celery, onion, garlic, and dill to the rendered fat; cook for 8-10 minutes, stirring occasionally. Add sherry; raise the heat. Cook until liquid is mostly evaporated, about 5 minutes.

5. Add roasted cauliflower, broth, nondairy milk, and bay leaves. Season with remaining 1 tablespoon kosher salt and ½ teaspoon pepper. Bring to a low boil. Reduce heat; simmer for 25-30 minutes.

6. Remove and discard bay leaves. Using an immersion blender, puree soup until smooth. Garnish with beef fry croutons.

FRENCH ONION AND SHORT RIB SOUP

Meat **YIELDS** *6-8 servings*

A meaty twist on a classic French recipe, this rich, wholesome soup is satisfying and downright delicious. Thank you, Daniella, for the inspiration.

2 lb	boneless short ribs
3 Tbsp	kosher salt, divided
½ tsp	black pepper, divided
1 tsp	chili powder
¼ cup	flour
2 Tbsp	onion soup mix
3 Tbsp	olive oil
4 large	onions, halved and sliced, divided
6 cups	water
½ cup	Marsala wine

1. In a medium bowl, place short ribs, 1 tablespoon kosher salt, ¼ teaspoon black pepper, and chili powder; toss to combine. Marinate meat 30 minutes.

2. Meanwhile, in an 8-quart pot, heat oil over medium-high heat. When oil is hot, add short ribs and 1 sliced onion. Allow meat to brown, about 3 minutes per side. Add 2 sliced onions; stir to combine. Lower heat to medium-low; allow meat to slow cook, stirring occasionally, for 1½ hours.

3. In a small bowl, combine flour, onion soup mix, remaining salt, and remaining pepper; set aside.

4. Add remaining onion to pot; slow cook for 15 minutes. Stir in flour mixture until it forms a roux (see Note on page 30). Add water and wine; stir well. Bring mixture to a boil; lower heat and simmer for 30 minutes.

TOMATO SAUSAGE SOUP

Meat   **YIELDS** *8-10 servings*

With the addition of sausage and vermicelli, this simple homemade soup made with basic ingredients is perfect for when you want a filling dish that's a complete meal.

3 Tbsp	olive oil
1½ cups	vermicelli (fine egg noodles)
1 medium	onion, diced
1 (12-oz.) package	Polish sausage *or* knockwurst
1 tsp	dried oregano
2 tsp	dried basil
1 Tbsp	kosher salt
¼ tsp	black pepper
2 (28-oz) cans	crushed tomatoes
5 cups	chicken stock *or* **5 cups** water **+ 2 Tbsp** consommé
½ cup	dry white wine

1. In an 8-quart pot, heat oil over medium heat. Toast vermicelli in hot oil, stirring occasionally, until golden. Remove with a slotted spoon; set aside.

2. Cut sausage into thick slices; add to oil remaining in pot. Fry until slightly colored. Remove with slotted spoon; set aside. Add onion to pot; sauté until translucent.

3. Add seasonings to pot; stir until aromatic, about 30 seconds. Add crushed tomatoes, chicken stock, and white wine. Return sausage to pot. Bring to a boil. Lower heat to a simmer. Simmer for 10 minutes. Add 1 cup vermicelli. Turn off heat; allow to rest 10 minutes.

4. Serve warm. Garnish with ½ cup toasted vermicelli.

Fish

SEARED TUNA PLATTER

Pareve   YIELDS *10-12 servings*

Seared tuna is a great way to serve fish to guests who might be hesitant about trying something new. Tuna has a delicious meaty flavor and the fabulous dipping sauce is a perfect accompaniment to this beautiful platter.

2-2 ½ lb	sushi grade tuna
¼ **cup**	Italian dressing
¼ **cup**	teriyaki sauce
¼	red onion, very finely diced, to garnish
1	jalapeño pepper, seeded and very finely diced, to garnish

Sweet Dipping Sauce

¼ **cup**	low sodium soy sauce
¼ **cup**	honey
2 Tbsp	mirin/Japanese sweet wine
2 cloves	garlic, crushed
1 tsp	toasted sesame oil

1. Cut tuna into 2-inch x 2½-inch x 5-inch chunks (see Note).

2. Combine Italian dressing and teriyaki sauce in a large resealable bag. Mix to combine. Add tuna chunks. Marinate for at least 1 hour in the refrigerator.

3. Coat a large skillet with cooking spray; place over medium-high heat to preheat. Place 2 tuna chunks into the hot skillet (hear the sizzle); sear each side for 1-2 minutes, depending on desired degree of doneness. Repeat with remaining tuna chunks.

4. Remove seared tuna chunks from skillet; allow to rest 10 minutes before cutting into ⅓-inch slices.

5. **Prepare the sweet dipping sauce:** In a small bowl, whisk together all dipping sauce ingredients until well combined. (Dipping sauce stays fresh in the refrigerator for 2 weeks in an airtight container.)

6. To serve, slightly overlap tuna slices around the serving tray. Serve with sweet dipping sauce. Garnish platter with red onion and jalapeño.

— Note

You can request that your fishmonger cut the tuna into these chunks.

MACADAMIA-CRUSTED SEA BASS WITH BALSAMIC REDUCTION

Pareve

YIELDS *8 main dish servings*

4 (1-inch-thick) sea bass center cut fillets, deboned and cut in half

- kosher salt, to taste
- black pepper, to taste

8 Tbsp duck sauce

¾ cup macadamia nuts, chopped

Balsamic Reduction

1 cup balsamic vinegar

2 Tbsp powdered sugar

The first time our friend, Chef Aryeh Goldenson, served this to me I KNEW I had to include it in my cookbook. The tartness of the balsamic reduction is the perfect pairing to this fabulous fish.

1. Preheat oven to 350°F. Line a baking sheet with parchment paper.

2. Rinse sea bass; pat dry. Season with salt and pepper.

3. Lightly coat a skillet with cooking spray; heat over high heat. Sear each fillet for 1-2 minutes on each side; transfer to prepared baking sheet. Bake, uncovered, for 10 minutes.

4. Remove from oven. Spread 1 tablespoon duck sauce on each fillet. Top with chopped macadamia nuts. Return to oven; bake 10 minutes. Remove from oven; allow to cool.

5. **Prepare the balsamic reduction:** In a small saucepan, bring balsamic vinegar to a boil. Lower heat; simmer for 20-25 minutes, until reduced vinegar lightly coats the back of a spoon. Remove from heat; stir in powdered sugar. Transfer mixture to a bowl; allow to cool. Mixture will thicken as it cools.

6. Once cool, drizzle each fillet with balsamic reduction before serving.

— Note —

This dish can be served as an appetizer; simply cut fillets into smaller portions before baking.

BROWN BUTTER BARRAMUNDI

Dairy YIELDS *4 servings*

Savory, light, and delicious, barramundi is a light, mild-flavored fish. It can be substituted with fluke, flounder, tilapia, halibut, or turbot.

2 (1½ lb)	barramundi fillets
½ tsp	kosher salt
¼ tsp	black pepper

Browned Butter Sauce

8 Tbsp	garlic butter (see Note)
2 Tbsp	freshly squeezed lemon juice

Crumb Topping

2 Tbsp	butter
¼ cup	seasoned panko crumbs
2 Tbsp	grated Parmesan cheese

1. **Prepare the browned butter sauce:** In a small saucepan over low heat, melt garlic butter. Simmer melted butter for 1-2 minutes until it begins to turn golden. Don't raise the heat. Watch pan carefully to avoid burning. (If using plain butter, brown the butter in a saucepan. Remove from heat and immediately add one clove crushed garlic. Swirl the pan and the garlic will become fragrant.) Add lemon juice to browned butter; set aside.

2. Preheat oven to 350°F. Line a baking pan with parchment paper.

3. Rinse fish; pat dry. Slice each fillet in half widthwise. Sprinkle fish with salt and pepper.

4. Arrange fish in prepared pan; cover with browned butter sauce. Wipe the saucepan (no need to wash it out).

5. **Prepare the crumb topping:** In the same saucepan, melt butter; add panko crumbs and Parmesan cheese. Stir until combined and slightly toasty. Remove from heat; divide the topping evenly over the barramundi. Place in the oven; bake for 12 minutes.

6. Transfer to a serving plate.

— Note —

To make your own garlic butter, mix together ½ cup softened butter and 1 clove crushed garlic.

POACHED MEDITERRANEAN FLOUNDER

Pareve YIELDS *4 servings*

Marinated eggplant is a top favorite of mine. Matbucha is the winner with my family. I came up with a way to make everyone happy with this Mediterranean-inspired flounder.

4 flounder fillets

Tomato Eggplant Sauce

1-2 Tbsp olive oil

1 baby eggplant, cut into 1-inch chunks

½ yellow bell pepper, sliced into ½-inch strips

½ red bell pepper, sliced into ½-inch strips

1 small onion, diced

2 cloves garlic, crushed

1 (15-oz) can fire-roasted diced tomatoes

1 (6-oz) can tomato paste

2 Tbsp lemon juice

1 Tbsp dark brown sugar

1 tsp kosher salt

¼ tsp black pepper

¼ tsp garlic powder

1 tsp paprika

1. **Prepare the tomato eggplant sauce:** In a large skillet, over medium heat, heat oil. Add eggplant; fry, stirring occasionally, for 10 minutes. Push eggplant to one side of the pan. Add peppers, onion, and garlic; cook for 5 minutes.

2. Add remaining sauce ingredients; stir to combine. Reduce heat to low. Cover pan; simmer for 10 minutes.

3. Uncover pan; place flounder fillets onto the tomato/eggplant sauce. Simmer, covered, for 15-20 minutes, until fish flakes easily. Serve fish topped with tomato/eggplant sauce.

— Tip —

When eggplants are in season and sweet, there is no need to pretreat them. Here is a method to remove any bitterness from eggplant: Place chunks of eggplant into a strainer, sprinkle with kosher salt, and allow to sit for 15-20 minutes. Rinse before using in a recipe.

Italian eggplants are long and thin and are rarely bitter, so although smaller in size than regular eggplants, they are a very good option.

HERBES DE PROVENCE
RED SNAPPER & VEGGIE SWIRLS

Pareve   YIELDS *3 servings*

This is a perfect, quick weeknight dinner. Total prep and cooking time is only 15 minutes! You'll have just enough time to prepare one more side and set your table. Then you can sit, relax, and enjoy this fabulous fast dish.

3	red snapper fillets
1 Tbsp	olive oil
1 (16-oz) package	spiralized yellow and green zucchini
5 cloves	garlic, crushed, divided
1 tsp	kosher salt, divided
½ tsp	black pepper, divided
1½ tsp	herbes de Provence, divided
½ tsp	garlic powder
1 cup	white wine
•	lemon wedges, for garnish

1. Rinse fish; pat dry.

2. Heat a large skillet over medium heat. Add oil, zucchini, 3 cloves garlic, ½ teaspoon salt, ¼ teaspoon black pepper, and ½ teaspoon herbes de Provence. Toss to combine.

3. Divide remaining 2 cloves crushed garlic evenly between the fillets. Sprinkle remaining spices over fish. Place fish, skin-side up, over vegetables. Pour wine over fish; allow mixture to cook, uncovered, for 12 minutes.

4. Carefully lift fish from the pan; plate skin-side down. Top with vegetable mixture. Serve warm. Garnish with lemon wedges.

— Variation —

Red snapper can be substituted with striped bass, tilapia, or flounder.

— Note —

Herbes de Provence is a dried herb blend of French origin. For a different but equally delicious flavor, substitute Italian seasoning or a dried herb mixture of your choice.

QUINOA-CRUSTED BRANZINO

Dairy **YIELDS** *4 servings*

Protein power packed, this quinoa branzino delivers perfection.

4	branzino fillets
¼ tsp	kosher salt
¼ tsp	black pepper
½ tsp	garlic powder
¼ cup	mayonnaise
2 Tbsp	Dijon mustard
1 tsp	yellow mustard
1 Tbsp	grated Parmesan cheese
1-1½ cups	cooked quinoa, chilled

1. Preheat oven to 425°F. Line a baking sheet with parchment paper; coat with cooking spray.

2. Rinse fish; pat dry. Arrange fillets in a single layer on prepared baking sheet. Season with salt, pepper, and garlic powder.

3. In a small bowl, stir together mayonnaise, mustards, and Parmesan until combined. Spread half the mayonnaise dressing over fillets. Sprinkle quinoa over dressing until fish is lightly coated.

4. Bake 15 minutes. Drizzle remaining dressing over baked fillets before serving. Serve warm.

Variation

Branzino can be substituted with fluke, flounder, or tilapia.

Note

Note that ½-¾ cup uncooked quinoa will yield 1-1½ cups cooked.

Tip

You can prep in advance for this recipe by making the quinoa the night before; reserve 1½ cups for the fish.

SALMON TERIYAKI

Pareve **YIELDS** *6 servings*

Over the years I have had my share of many different versions of salmon teriyaki. After tasting this one, I have never tried another. Thanks to my friend Batsheva for this winner.

6 (1¼-inch -thick) salmon fillets

- sea salt, to taste
- onion powder, to taste
- garlic powder, to taste
- paprika, to taste

⅓ cup teriyaki sauce

⅓ cup seasoned breadcrumbs

¼ cup honey

½ cup slivered almonds *or* honey-glazed slivered almonds

1. Preheat oven to 350°F. Prepare a 9x13-inch pan.

2. Wash salmon fillets; pat dry. Arrange in prepared pan; lightly sprinkle with salt, onion powder, garlic powder, and paprika. Drizzle teriyaki sauce over fillets. Sprinkle evenly with seasoned breadcrumbs. Drizzle with honey. Sprinkle with slivered almonds.

3. Bake for 20 minutes. Serve warm or at room temperature.

— Note
You can substitute any spice blend of your choice.

HONEY MUSTARD SALMON WITH PRETZEL CRUMB TOPPING

Pareve   YIELDS *6-8 servings*

Pretzels and mustard are a perfect pair and my inspiration for this recipe. Together they remind me of a delicious hot pretzel treat. They add great taste and texture to this prize-winning salmon.

1 (2-3-lb) side   salmon

- sea salt, to taste
- onion powder, to taste
- garlic powder, to taste
- paprika, to taste
- black pepper, to taste

Honey Mustard Sauce

2 Tbsp   Dijon mustard, preferably stone ground

2 Tbsp   honey *or* silan

1 Tbsp   apple cider vinegar

1 Tbsp   olive oil

1 clove   garlic, crushed

¼ tsp   sea salt

⅛ tsp   black pepper

Pretzel Crumb Topping

¼ cup   seasoned panko crumbs

¼ cup   pretzel crumbs

1 Tbsp   fresh parsley, chopped *or* dried parsley flakes

- lemon wedges, for garnish, optional
- fresh parsley, for garnish, optional
- pretzel crisps, crushed (not ground), optional

1. Preheat oven to 400°F. Line a baking sheet with parchment paper; coat with cooking spray.

2. Rinse salmon; pat dry. Place on prepared baking sheet. Season lightly with spices.

3. **Prepare the honey mustard sauce:** In a small bowl, combine sauce ingredients. Spread sauce over salmon.

4. **Prepare the pretzel crumb topping:** In a small bowl, combine topping ingredients. Sprinkle over honey mustard sauce, to coat.

5. Bake 35-40 minutes, uncovered, until fish flakes easily.

6. Garnish with lemon wedges, fresh parsley, and crushed (not ground) pretzel crisps, if desired.

— Variation

This recipe can be made using salmon fillets; bake for 15-20 minutes.

MAPLE-BARBECUE SALMON

Pareve YIELDS *8 servings*

You won't have to fish for compliments when you serve this flavorful fish! This is one of my personal favorites. The glaze gives the salmon a bold yet sweet flavor. Try it and you'll understand why this has become a true classic in our family.

8 (1¼-inch -thick) salmon fillets

- sea salt, to taste
- onion powder, to taste
- garlic powder, to taste
- paprika, to taste

Maple-Barbecue Sauce

1 bunch scallions, white and light green parts only, sliced

½ cup pure maple syrup

¼ cup barbecue sauce

2 Tbsp apple cider vinegar

1 tsp balsamic vinegar, optional

1 Tbsp yellow mustard

1. Preheat oven to 400°F. Line a baking sheet with parchment paper.

2. **Prepare the maple-barbecue sauce:** In a small saucepan, stir together all sauce ingredients. Over medium-low heat, bring the mixture to a boil; remove from heat.

3. Rinse salmon fillets; pat dry. Arrange fish on prepared baking sheet, making sure not to crowd the slices. Season lightly with spices.

4. Brush salmon with sauce. Bake for 10 minutes. Baste with sauce; bake for 10 minutes. Remove from oven; baste again before serving.

— Note —
You can substitute any spice blend of your choice.

SNAPPY LEMON AND GARLIC SALMON

Pareve or Dairy

YIELDS *4 servings*

4 (1-inch)	center cut salmon fillets, skin removed
2 Tbsp	butter *or* cooking spray

Snappy Lemon and Garlic Rub

5 Tbsp	paprika
5 Tbsp	lemon pepper mix (see Note)
3½ Tbsp	garlic powder
1 tsp	crushed red pepper flakes, or to taste
3 Tbsp	dried thyme
3 Tbsp	dried oregano
3 Tbsp	onion powder
2¼ tsp	ground mustard

Tartar Sauce

1 cup	mayonnaise
3 Tbsp	finely diced red onion
1 Tbsp	lemon juice
2 tsp	sweet relish
¼ tsp	sea salt
⅛ tsp	black pepper
•	lemon wedges, for serving

Robust and full of flavor, this lemon and garlic rub can be prepped and stored for three months in an airtight container. I love it on any fish, but is also terrific rubbed on chicken before broiling.

1. Preheat oven to high broil. Line a baking sheet with parchment paper.

2. **Prepare the snappy lemon and garlic rub:** In a resealable bag or airtight container combine rub ingredients; mix well.

3. Rinse fish; pat dry. Using a very sharp knife, cut each fillet into 5 (1-inch) cubes. Place ¼-cup prepared rub into a bowl, adding more if necessary. Roll salmon cubes in rub to coat well. Place salmon on prepared baking sheet. Top each cube with a dot of butter or coat with cooking spray. Broil for 5 minutes.

4. **Prepare the tartar sauce:** In a small bowl, stir together sauce ingredients until well combined.

5. Serve salmon with tartar sauce and a lemon wedge. Salmon cubes may be skewered.

Variation

This recipe can be prepared with salmon fillets. Coat fillets with prepared rub; broil for 7 minutes.

Notes

Make your own lemon pepper by combining equal parts lemon zest and black pepper.

You can increase the number of salmon cubes as needed; the broiling time remains the same.

Poultry

OVEN SOUTHERN FRIED CHICKEN

Meat YIELDS *4 servings*

Crispy, juicy, and tender, this all-American classic is baked to perfection.

12	chicken drumsticks, skin on
1⅓ cups	flour
1 Tbsp	garlic powder
1 Tbsp	kosher salt
1 tsp	onion powder
1 tsp	chili powder
1 tsp	paprika
1 tsp	black pepper
¼-½ tsp	turmeric
2	eggs
1-2 tsp	hot sauce, such as Frank's
1 tsp	yellow mustard
½ cup (1 stick)	margarine, melted

1. Coat a baking sheet with cooking spray.

2. **Prepare the coating mixtures:** Place flour and spices into a resealable bag. Using a fork, beat eggs in a medium bowl; stir in hot sauce and mustard.

3. Place drumsticks into bag of flour mixture; shake to coat chicken. Dip each drumstick into egg mixture, then shake in flour mixture again.

4. Place drumsticks onto prepared baking sheet. Drizzle 1 tablespoon melted margarine over each drumstick (it's OK if it runs down the sides). Refrigerate for 30 minutes.

5. Preheat oven to 400°F.

6. Bake chicken on center rack for 45-50 minutes, until juices run clear when chicken is pierced with a fork.

CRANBERRY CHICKEN SHEET PAN DINNER

Meat   YIELDS *4 servings*

Sheet pan suppers take the stress out of the everyday question, "What should I make tonight?" Here is a well-balanced, all in one, WINNER of a dinner.

8-10   chicken drumsticks

4 small   sweet potatoes, peeled and sliced into French-fry-style strips

•   olive oil

•   kosher salt, to taste

•   black pepper, to taste

1 (10.5-oz) bag   frozen edamame in pods (may substitute green beans)

Cranberry Dressing

½ cup   jellied cranberry sauce, mashed with a fork

2 Tbsp   Dijon mustard

¼ cup   pure maple syrup

2 Tbsp   chili sauce *or* ketchup

2 Tbsp   apple cider vinegar

1. Preheat oven to 475°F. Line 2 baking sheets with parchment paper; coat with cooking spray.

2. Place 4-5 drumsticks at the center of each sheet. Arrange sweet potato strips on either side of drumsticks. Drizzle drumsticks and fries with olive oil, salt, and pepper. Toss fries to coat evenly, leaving room on the baking sheet for the edamame (Step 5).

3. Bake, uncovered, for 40 minutes.

4. **Prepare the cranberry dressing:** Combine dressing ingredients in a small pot; bring to a boil over medium heat. Stir until smooth. Alternatively, microwave the mixture for 2 minutes, stirring once after 1 minute.

5. Remove baking sheets from the oven. Brush drumsticks with dressing. Toss edamame with olive oil, salt, and pepper; place next to the sweet potato fries.

6. Return baking sheets to the oven, rotating top sheet to bottom shelf and bottom sheet to top shelf. Bake for 10 minutes.

7. Remove baking sheets from oven. Brush drumsticks with dressing again. Bake for 10 minutes.

HONEY-GARLIC CHICKEN

Meat   YIELDS *4 servings*

Bored of all your ho-hum chicken on-the-bone recipes? On the lookout for something new? This great one is definitely a keeper.

4	chicken quarters (tops and/or bottoms)
½ tsp	kosher salt
¼ tsp	black pepper
½ tsp	onion powder
½ tsp	garlic powder
1 tsp	paprika

Dressing

1 Tbsp	olive oil
1 small	shallot, sliced
1 clove	garlic, crushed
½ cup	honey
2 Tbsp	ketchup
2 Tbsp	lemon juice
¼ tsp	sea salt
¼ tsp	ground mustard
⅛ tsp	chili powder
⅛ tsp	black pepper

1. Preheat oven to 350°F. Set out a 9x13-inch baking pan.

2. Place chicken pieces in prepared baking pan.

3. In a small bowl, combine all spices; lightly season chicken. Cover baking pan with foil. Bake for 1 hour.

4. **Prepare the dressing:** In a small saucepan over medium heat, heat olive oil; add shallot and garlic. Sauté until softened, 5-8 minutes. Stir in remaining ingredients until combined. Remove from heat.

5. Remove chicken from oven; drain liquid from pan (see Note).

6. Spoon dressing evenly over the chicken. Return pan to oven; bake for 30 minutes, uncovered.

— Note
Discard drained liquid after it has cooled.

SAVORY HERB-RUBBED CHICKEN

Meat   YIELDS *8 servings*

For amazingly moist chicken, you may add an easy step called brining prior to baking (Step 1). Brining the chicken helps it absorb the spices and flavors. If you are short on time, however, simply begin with Step 2.

2 (2½ 3-lb)	chickens, cut into quarters or eighths
2-3 Tbsp	honey

Savory Herb Rub

9 Tbsp	dark brown sugar (packed)
6 Tbsp	sweet or smoked paprika
4½ Tbsp	chili powder
3 Tbsp	kosher salt
3 tsp	garlic powder
2¼ tsp	black pepper
1½ tsp	cumin
¾ tsp	crushed red pepper flakes
¾ tsp	nutmeg

Optional Brining Liquid

4 cups	water
⅓ cup	dark brown sugar
⅓ cup	kosher salt
⅓ cup	vinegar

1. **Optional: Brine the chicken:** Fill a large container with brining liquid ingredients. Mix all together. Add chicken; marinate, covered, in refrigerator for at least one hour or overnight.

2. **Prepare the savory herb rub:** In a small bowl, mix together rub ingredients.

3. Preheat oven to 350°F. Prepare a 9x13-inch baking pan.

4. Remove chicken from brine, if using. Pat chicken dry; coat generously with rub. Cover; bake for 1 hour 15 minutes. Uncover; drizzle with honey. Broil for five minutes.

— Note

Leftover savory herb rub can be stored for 3 months in an airtight container.

SWEET CHILI-GLAZED CHICKEN WINGS

Meat   YIELDS *6 servings*

Finger-lickin' good!

2 lb	chicken wings
3 Tbsp	olive oil
1 Tbsp	kosher salt
½ tsp	black pepper

Sweet Chili Glaze

½ cup	honey
½ cup	sweet chili sauce
5 cloves	garlic, crushed
3 Tbsp	low sodium soy sauce
3 Tbsp	apple cider vinegar
¼-½ tsp	crushed red pepper flakes, or to taste

1. Preheat oven to 450°F. Set out a baking sheet.

2. Pat wings dry with a paper towel (this will help crisp the skin). Place wings on prepared baking sheet. Drizzle with olive oil; sprinkle with salt and pepper. Turn wings to coat evenly.

3. Bake skin-side up, uncovered, for 20 minutes.

4. **Prepare the sweet chili glaze:** In a small bowl, combine glaze ingredients.

5. Remove wings from oven. Pour off any liquid. Turn wings over. Pour glaze over wings. Bake for 15 minutes. Brush wings with glaze from the baking sheet. Bake for another 15 minutes.

6. Turn wings skin-side up. Brush wings once again with glaze. Raise oven temperature to 500°F. Bake an additional 10-15 minutes. Wings will have a fabulous BBQ look.

DUCK BREAST WITH BLACKBERRY SAUCE

Meat   YIELDS *4 servings*

Duck breast is an underutilized delicacy. This recipe is easy to prepare and creates a beautiful showpiece entree for your family and guests. It's a welcome change from chicken and beef.

4   duck breasts, chilled
•   kosher salt, to taste
•   black pepper, to taste

Blackberry Sauce

⅓ cup   blackberry preserves
1 Tbsp   red wine vinegar
½ Tbsp   hot water
•   kosher salt, to taste
•   black pepper, to taste

1. Preheat oven to 400°F. Set out a 9x13-inch baking pan.

2. Score chilled duck breast skin in a crosshatch pattern. Season both sides with salt and pepper. Place duck breast, skin-side down, into a cold skillet. Turn the heat to medium-high; allow the fat to begin rendering as the skin begins to become crispy, about 4 minutes. Turn breasts over; crisp second side 3-4 minutes. Remove from heat.

3. Transfer duck breasts to prepared baking pan, skin-side down. Place into oven; roast for 6-8 minutes.

4. Allow duck to rest 5 minutes before slicing. Serve with blackberry sauce.

5. **Prepare the blackberry sauce:** In a small bowl, whisk together blackberry preserves and red wine vinegar. Add water, a little at a time, until the right consistency is reached. If preserves are very thin, less water may be needed. Sauce should have a thickened consistency. Add salt and pepper, to taste.

—Tips—

How to know that your duck is ready? Press down on the center; if there is give and it still has a bounce to it, it will be pink in the center. Do not allow to become solid and hard to touch; that means it is overdone and has lost its juiciness.

You may save the duck fat for future use. It has absolutely delicious flavor. (Great to fry spuds, etc.)

CHICKEN ROLL-UPS WITH ROASTED RED PEPPER CHUTNEY

Meat YIELDS *8 servings*

The medley of colors combined with the downright delicious flavors put this chicken roll-up in a category of its own.

8 chicken cutlets, thinly sliced

Marinade

¼ cup olive oil

3 Tbsp lemon juice

1 Tbsp dried parsley flakes

1 tsp consommé powder

1 tsp black pepper

1 tsp Dijon mustard

¾ tsp sea salt

Quinoa, Spinach, and Onion Filling

1 Tbsp olive oil

1 cube frozen sautéed onion (see Note page 70)

1 clove garlic, crushed

½ cup raw quinoa

1 cup chicken broth *or* **1 cup** hot water + **1 Tbsp** consommé powder

• sea salt, to taste

• black pepper, to taste

¼ cup chopped frozen spinach, thawed and squeezed dry

1. Combine marinade ingredients in a large resealable bag. Shake to mix well. Add chicken cutlets; turn to completely coat all the pieces with the marinade. Refrigerate overnight.

2. **Prepare the quinoa, spinach, and onion filling:** In a medium frying pan, heat oil over medium heat. Add frozen onion cube and garlic; sauté for 1-2 minutes. Add raw quinoa, chicken broth, salt, and pepper. Bring to a boil. Cover pan, lower heat, and simmer for 15 minutes. Remove from heat; allow mixture to rest, covered, for 5 minutes. Remove lid; fluff quinoa with a fork. Add spinach. Stir together until fully combined.

3. **Assemble the roll-ups:** Preheat oven to 350°F. Coat a baking dish with cooking spray or a small amount of oil.

4. Remove 1 cutlet from the marinade; place it on a flat surface. Top with 1-2 tablespoons filling; spread filling over the entire cutlet. Roll up and seal with a toothpick, then place seam-side down in prepared baking dish. Repeat with remaining cutlets and filling.

5. Bake, uncovered, for 30 minutes. Serve with Roasted Red Pepper Chutney (recipe follows).

— Variation

Prepare chicken cutlets without the stuffing and serve with the red pepper chutney. The chutney is very flavorful and simple to make; it freezes beautifully and can be used in many different ways.

ROASTED RED PEPPER CHUTNEY

2	red bell peppers
2 Tbsp	olive oil
1	shallot, minced
3 Tbsp	white wine
6 Tbsp	chicken stock, *or* **6 Tbsp** water + **1 tsp** consommé powder
3 Tbsp	lemon juice
½ tsp	sea salt
⅛ tsp	black pepper

1. Preheat oven to 400°F.

2. Place whole peppers on a baking sheet; roast until skin puckers and flesh is soft, about 45 minutes. Remove peppers from the oven; place into a bowl. Cover the bowl with plastic wrap; set aside for 10 minutes to allow the peppers to "sweat." Peel peppers; cut in half. Discard skin and seeds. Slice the roasted peppers; set aside.

3. Heat oil in a small saucepan over medium heat. Add shallot; sauté until soft. Add white wine. Cook, stirring, for 1 minute. Add peppers and chicken stock; cook for 5 minutes. Cool slightly. Use an immersion blender to puree mixture. Season with lemon juice, salt, and pepper. Reheat over low heat when ready to use.

—Note—

If short on time, instead of oven-roasting the peppers, you can roast them over an open flame, slowly turning the peppers. After the skin puckers and flesh is soft, follow above directions.

Poultry

CASHEW AND BROCCOLI STIR FRY

Meat **YIELDS** *4-5 servings*

My daughter watched as I whipped up this dish; she tasted it and exclaimed, "This should be called Fab in 20!" Indeed, it's a one-pan absolutely fabulous dinner.

1½ Tbsp	sesame oil, divided
1 lb	chicken cutlets, sliced into strips
4 cloves	garlic, crushed
1	onion, sliced
½ lb (8-oz)	broccoli florets
6 oz	mushrooms, quartered
½	red bell pepper, sliced into 1-inch matchsticks
3 Tbsp	honey
4½ Tbsp	hoisin sauce
1½ Tbsp	water
1½ Tbsp	apple cider vinegar
1 tsp	cornstarch
¼ tsp	ground ginger
½ cup	cashews, roasted or honey roasted

1. In a large frying pan over medium heat, heat 1 tablespoon sesame oil. Add chicken strips and garlic. Stir constantly until chicken is cooked through. Transfer to a bowl; set aside.

2. Add ½ tablespoon sesame oil to the same frying pan. Raise heat to medium-high. Add onion; stir fry for 4 minutes. Add broccoli, mushrooms, and pepper; stir fry until soft.

3. Meanwhile, in a medium bowl, combine honey, hoisin sauce, water, apple cider vinegar, cornstarch, and ginger; whisk until smooth.

4. Return chicken to the pan; pour in sauce. Stir constantly until mixture boils and thickens, about 2 minutes. Stir in cashews.

5. Serve immediately.

SWEET HEAT BATTER-DIPPED CHICKEN NUGGETS

Meat   YIELDS *4-6 servings*

These are not your same old chicken poppers. With the sweet heat batter, every single bite is an explosion of flavor.

1½-2 lb	chicken tenders, cut into chunks or nuggets
½ cup	cornflake crumbs, optional
•	oil, for frying

Batter

1 cup	flour
1 tsp	paprika
1 tsp	sea salt
1 tsp	garlic powder
½ tsp	baking powder
2	eggs
¼ cup	honey
¼ cup	nondairy milk *or* water
2 Tbsp	hot sauce, such as Frank's

Roasted Garlic

1 head	garlic
1 Tbsp	olive oil
•	kosher salt, for sprinkling
pinch	black pepper

Roasted Garlic Aioli Sauce

•	Roasted Garlic, above
½ cup	mayonnaise
1 tsp	kosher salt
1 tsp	lemon juice
⅛ tsp	black pepper
dash	fish-free Worcestershire Sauce

1. **Prepare the roasted garlic:** Preheat oven to 350°F.

2. Slice off top of the garlic head. Place garlic head on a piece of foil large enough to enclose garlic. Drizzle with olive oil; sprinkle with salt and pepper. Seal garlic in foil; roast for 30-40 minutes.

3. **Prepare the roasted garlic aioli sauce:** Squeeze roasted garlic cloves out of the peels into a small bowl. Add remaining sauce ingredients. Puree with an immersion blender.

4. **Prepare the batter-dipped chicken nuggets:** In a large skillet over medium-high heat, heat 1½-inches oil.

5. Working quickly, combine all dry batter ingredients in a medium-sized bowl. Add wet ingredients; whisk until a smooth batter forms. Add chicken nuggets; toss to coat well.

6. Optional: Place cornflake crumbs onto a platter. Roll batter-dipped chicken in cornflake crumbs.

7. Add coated chicken nuggets to hot oil; fry until golden, turning once, 3-4 minutes per side.

8. Transfer fried nuggets to a paper towel-lined colander to drain excess oil.

9. Serve with Roasted Garlic Aioli Sauce. You may substitute duck sauce, if desired.

—Note

Additional serving suggestions for the Roasted Garlic Aioli Sauce:
Serve alongside Beef Fry and Onion-Filled Hamburgers, p. 188.
Serve with Fully Loaded Veggie Burgers, p. 50.
Serve alongside any roast.
Use as a dip.

GENERAL TSO'S CHICKEN AND BROCCOLI BAKE

Meat YIELDS *4-6 servings*

A true Chinese classic that tastes like the real deal. Your family will keep requesting this no-fuss, simple, easy, and delicious dinner.

1½ lb	chicken cutlets, cut into strips
¼ cup	flour
1 tsp	kosher salt
⅛ tsp	black pepper
24 oz	frozen broccoli florets, defrosted
½-1 cup	honey-glazed cashews
•	black and white sesame seeds, for sprinkling, optional

General Tso's Sauce

⅓ cup	sugar
2 Tbsp	cornstarch
½ cup	water
⅓ cup	rice vinegar
⅓ cup	low sodium soy sauce
1½ Tbsp	hoisin sauce
4 cloves	garlic, crushed
½ tsp	ground ginger
¼-½ tsp	crushed red pepper flakes

1. Preheat oven to 350°F. Coat a 9x13-inch baking pan with cooking spray.

2. Place chicken strips, flour, salt, and pepper into a resealable bag. Seal bag; shake until all chicken strips are well coated. Remove strips from flour. Shake off the excess flour; place chicken strips into prepared baking pan.

3. **Prepare the General Tso's sauce:** In a small saucepan, whisk together sugar and cornstarch. Whisk in water. Add remaining ingredients; whisk until smooth. Bring to a boil over medium-high heat, stirring constantly. Lower heat to a simmer and allow sauce to thicken, until it lightly coats the back of spoon. Remove from heat. Alternatively, place mixture into a microwave-safe bowl or container. Microwave on high for 1 minute; stir well. Repeat this two more times for a total of 3 minutes in the microwave. Mixture will be smooth and thickened.

4. Pour half the sauce over the chicken strips. Cover pan with foil; bake for 30 minutes.

5. Remove pan from oven. Place broccoli florets over the chicken strips. Pour remaining sauce over the broccoli. Cover; bake an additional 15-20 minutes.

6. Before serving, sprinkle with glazed cashews and sesame seeds, if using.

SIMPLE SUPPER

MARINATED GRILLED CHICKEN

Meat YIELDS *6-8 servings*

2 lb chicken cutlets

Marinade

3 Tbsp mayonnaise

2 Tbsp pure maple syrup

1 Tbsp Dijon mustard

3 cloves garlic, crushed

½ tsp kosher salt

½ tsp black pepper

½ tsp dried basil

¼ tsp dried oregano

1 Tbsp apple cider vinegar

3 Tbsp dried parsley flakes

My friend Chani was helping me test recipes. Her children are picky eaters and don't usually like chicken. When they tasted this one, they declared it "best chicken ever!"

1. **Prepare the marinade:** Combine all marinade ingredients in a resealable bag.

2. Add cutlets to marinade; turn to coat well. Marinate for at least 20 minutes or up to overnight.

3. Heat a large grill pan or skillet over medium-high heat. Coat with cooking spray and allow to begin to smoke. Grill chicken 4-5 minutes per side until cooked through.

— Note —

This can also be prepared on an indoor or outdoor grill, or broiled in the oven; the cooking time will be the same.

To reheat, wrap chicken in foil, place wrapped chicken into a baking pan. Cover with foil and warm in a warming drawer or on the inverted cover of a slow cooker. The double wrapping will prevent loss of moisture.

CREAMY PESTO CHICKEN

Meat   YIELDS *8 servings*

I love the flavor of this homemade pesto and the way it takes chicken to the next level. In fact, I enjoy the pesto so much that I serve it as a Shabbos dip, toss it with pasta, and even use it to top grilled vegetables.

8 thinly sliced chicken cutlets

1 cup seasoned panko crumbs

1 cup shelled salted pistachio nuts, crushed

2-3 Tbsp honey, for drizzling

Creamy Pesto

1 cup mayonnaise

1 cup fresh basil leaves *or* **12** frozen basil cubes

4 cloves garlic

2 Tbsp vinegar

2 tsp honey

1½ tsp sea salt

1 tsp black pepper

1. Preheat oven to 350°F. Line a baking sheet with parchment paper; coat with cooking spray.

2. **Prepare the pesto:** In a medium bowl, use an immersion blender to combine mayonnaise, basil, garlic, vinegar, honey, salt, and pepper until completely blended.

3. **Prepare the chicken:** In a medium bowl, stir together panko crumbs and crushed pistachios.

4. Dip each cutlet into the pesto, turning to thinly coat both sides. Next, dip coated cutlets into crumb mixture, turning and pressing lightly to coat completely.

5. Place coated cutlets onto prepared baking sheet; lightly coat with cooking spray. Drizzle with honey.

6. Bake, uncovered, for 30 minutes, until golden.

—Variation

This recipe also works with other types of chicken, such as thicker chicken cutlets or chicken on the bone. Bake thicker chicken cutlets, for 35 minutes. Bake chicken on the bone for 1 hour 10 minutes.

APRICOT-MUSTARD GLAZED CHICKEN

Meat   YIELDS *6 servings*

While prepping for Yom Tov and organizing my menu, I find myself time and time again including this sweet-and-sour apricot mustard chicken. With its ease of preparation and beautiful presentation, it's a no-brainer for me.

6 chicken cutlets
(not thinly sliced)

½ tsp kosher salt

½ tsp onion powder

½ tsp garlic powder

1 tsp paprika

• scallions, for garnish, optional

Apricot-Mustard Glaze

1 Tbsp olive oil

1 large shallot, finely diced

2 cloves garlic, crushed

½ cup apricot jam

⅓ cup apple cider vinegar

2 Tbsp water

½ tsp dried thyme

½ tsp Dijon mustard

1 Tbsp whole grain (coarsely ground) mustard

1½ Tbsp honey

½ tsp sea salt

½ tsp black pepper

1. Preheat oven to 350°F. Set out a 9x13-inch baking pan.

2. Arrange cutlets in prepared baking pan. Season lightly with spices.

3. **Prepare the apricot-mustard glaze:** In a small saucepan, heat olive oil over low heat. Add shallot; sauté for 5 minutes. Add crushed garlic; sauté 2 minutes. Add apricot jam, vinegar, water, thyme, both mustards, honey, salt, and pepper. Bring to a boil; reduce heat and simmer for 5-7 minutes.

4. Pour glaze over seasoned chicken; bake, uncovered, for 30 minutes.

5. Garnish with diced scallions, if desired.

Variation

This glaze works well with chicken on the bone. Spice chicken, cover with foil, and bake for 45 minutes at 350 °F. Remove chicken from oven, pour off juices, top with glaze, and bake, uncovered, for 45 minutes.

CHICKEN SCALOPPINI

Meat   YIELDS *6-8 servings*

1 lb **(10 slices)**	chicken cutlets, extra-thinly sliced
⅓ cup	cornstarch
¾ tsp	kosher salt
¼ tsp	black pepper
¼ cup	extra-light olive oil
1 small	onion, diced
3 cloves	garlic, crushed
1 cup	chicken stock *or* **1 cup** water + **1½ tsp** consommé powder
½ cup	semisweet white wine
1 tsp	dried rosemary, crushed, *or* **3** sprigs fresh rosemary, *or* **1 Tbsp** fresh rosemary, chopped
2½ Tbsp	fresh lemon juice
2 Tbsp	capers, drained

When I was asked at the last minute to make the Purim seudah for my son's entire chevrah, I needed an idea that would be beautiful and feed the hungry crowd. Chicken scaloppini proved to be a perfect choice that I now use regularly for family dinner.

1. On a small plate, combine cornstarch, salt, and pepper. Set aside.

2. Heat oil in a large frying pan. Add onion and garlic; sauté over medium heat for 5 minutes. Use a slotted spoon to remove onion and garlic from the pan; set aside.

3. Dredge chicken in the seasoned cornstarch mixture. Fry cutlets in the same frying pan over medium-high heat for 2-3 minutes on each side, until cooked through. Remove cutlets from pan and place on a serving tray.

4. Return onion/garlic mixture to the frying pan. Raise heat; deglaze pan by scraping the bottom occasionally until the mixture becomes light golden. Add chicken stock, wine, rosemary, lemon juice, and capers.

5. Bring mixture to a rolling boil, then lower heat to medium-high. Boil for 10 minutes, until the liquid reduces and thickens slightly. Pour mixture over chicken before serving.

Meat

DRUNKEN STEW AND DUMPLINGS

These super-easy dumplings are a perfect finishing touch that transforms this dish into an all-in-one meal. Guaranteed, your house will be filled with a fabulous aroma and your family will hardly be able to wait for dinner to be served.

Meat **YIELDS** *6 servings*

¼ cup	cornstarch
¼ cup	french fried onions, crushed
1 tsp	sea salt
½ tsp	black pepper
2 tsp	paprika
2 lb	beef stew cubes
3 Tbsp	olive oil
3	onions, sliced
4-5 cloves	garlic, crushed
2	sweet potatoes, cubed
1 (3.5-oz) package	shiitake mushrooms, sliced
1 (12-oz) bottle/can	beer
3¼ cups	beef broth *or* **3¼ cups** water + **3 Tbsp** beef broth powder
¼ cup	red wine vinegar
2	bay leaves
2 tsp	dried thyme
2 tsp	fish-free Worcestershire sauce
½ tsp	black pepper
3 Tbsp	dark brown sugar

Dumplings

1 cup	flour
2 tsp	baking powder
½ tsp	sea salt
2 Tbsp	canola oil
½ cup	water
2 Tbsp	fresh chives, chopped, optional

1. Preheat oven to 325°F.

2. In a large resealable bag, combine cornstarch, french fried onions, salt, pepper, and paprika. Add beef cubes; shake vigorously to coat.

3. In a large ovenproof skillet, over medium-high heat, heat oil. Add onions and meat. Sear meat and onions, turning occasionally, until meat is browned on all sides. Add garlic, sweet potatoes, and mushrooms. Stir until combined.

4. Stir in remaining ingredients; bring to a boil. Turn off heat, cover skillet, and transfer to preheated oven. Bake for 2 hours.

5. **Prepare the dumplings:** In a small bowl, combine all dumpling ingredients, stirring with a wooden spoon until batter reaches a sticky consistency.

6. Remove stew from oven; drop teaspoons of batter into stew (use a second spoon to push batter off). Cover; return to oven for 30 minutes.

7. Remove and discard bay leaves before serving.

GARLIC-MAYO SKIRT STEAK DINNER

Meat **YIELDS** *4 servings*

1½ lb skirt steak

1 lb multicolored baby potatoes

1 (10-oz) package greenhouse-grown broccoli

• olive oil

• kosher salt

• black pepper

Garlic-Mayo Dressing

6 Tbsp mayonnaise

2 cloves garlic, crushed

1 Tbsp vinegar

• kosher salt, to taste

• black pepper, to taste

dash hot sauce, optional

Sheet pan dinners are an excellent way to cut back on the time you spend preparing family meals. I love how quickly this whole meal bakes in one pan. It is finished in less than 30 minutes, with absolutely delicious flavors.

1. Preheat oven to 450°F. Set out a baking sheet.

2. Soak skirt steak in a bowl of cold water for 10 minutes to extract excess salt.

3. Meanwhile, place potatoes into a small saucepan. Cover with water; bring to a boil. Boil for 3-5 minutes, drain, and place along one long side of prepared baking sheet.

4. Slice skirt steak into 4-inch pieces; place next to the potatoes. Add broccoli in a single layer next to the meat. Drizzle meat, potatoes, and broccoli with olive oil; sprinkle with salt and pepper. Toss veggies to coat evenly. Cover; bake for 20 minutes.

5. **Prepare the garlic-mayo dressing:** Combine dressing ingredients in a small bowl; set aside.

6. Remove baking sheet from oven. Spread dressing over meat, potatoes, and broccoli.

7. Raise oven temperature to broil. Broil, uncovered, for 5 minutes.

CRISPY ORANGE BEEF

Meat **YIELDS** *4 servings*

1½ tsp	baking soda
3 Tbsp	water
1 lb	pepper steak, thinly sliced
1	egg white, lightly beaten
¼ cup	cornstarch
•	oil, for frying

Orange Sauce

3 Tbsp	dark brown sugar
2 Tbsp	sherry *or* rice vinegar
2 Tbsp	red wine vinegar
2 Tbsp	low sodium soy sauce
2 tsp	cornstarch
1 tsp	orange zest
¼ cup	orange juice
3 cloves	garlic, crushed
1 Tbsp	sweet chili sauce
⅛ tsp	ground ginger

On busy weeknights when I'm tempted to get takeout, this is the recipe I've turned to time and time again. It whips up in a matter of minutes. The sticky orange sauce is irresistible! You'll definitely want to make plenty of rice to serve with the extra sauce.

1. In a medium bowl, combine baking soda and water. Add pepper steak; stir to coat. Allow the mixture to rest for 15 minutes to tenderize the meat.

2. **Prepare the orange sauce:** Combine brown sugar, vinegars, soy sauce, and cornstarch in a small bowl. Whisk until smooth. Add zest, orange juice, garlic, sweet chili sauce, and ginger. Mix to combine. Set aside.

3. Add egg white and cornstarch to the meat mixture; toss to coat meat well.

4. Line a 9x13-inch pan with paper towels. Set aside.

5. Fill a large skillet with 1½-inches oil. Heat oil over medium-high heat. Add strips of meat, 1 piece at a time, to the hot oil; fry without moving strips until they begin to look crispy or float to the top, about 1 minute. Using a wide slotted spoon, transfer meat to prepared pan.

6. Pour off all but 1 tablespoon oil. Add orange sauce to the skillet; bring to a boil until thickened. Return crispy beef to the skillet; stir fry until meat is well coated with sauce.

—Tip—
This dish pairs well with cooked rice.

DECONSTRUCTED MEATBALLS

Meat **YIELDS** *6-8 servings*

2 Tbsp	olive oil
1 large	onion, diced
2 cloves	garlic, crushed
2-2½ lb	ground beef
1 (14.5-oz) can	fire-roasted diced tomatoes
½ cup	ketchup
½ cup	water
½ cup	finely diced sundried tomatoes (optional, but recommended)
2 Tbsp	dark brown sugar
1-2 Tbsp	hot sauce, such as Frank's
1 Tbsp	yellow mustard
2 tsp	chili powder
1 tsp	fish-free Worcestershire sauce

Short on time? You can serve this flavor-packed dinner on a bun or over rice, mashed potatoes, or good old-fashioned pasta. Best of all? An awesome dinner in just 30 minutes.

1. In a large saucepan, heat oil over medium heat. Add onion and garlic; sauté for 5 minutes until they begin to turn translucent. Add beef, stirring and breaking apart large lumps as it browns.

2. Add diced tomatoes, ketchup, water, and sundried tomatoes. Stir until combined. Add remaining ingredients. Stir until totally incorporated.

3. Lower heat; cover and cook for 20 minutes.

4. Remove cover. Raise heat; stir and cook until most of the liquid has cooked off.

BEEF FRY AND ONION-FILLED BURGERS

Meat **YIELDS** *22-24 patties*

Make sure you have plenty of these prepared when you serve these outrageous burgers! They are just bursting with deliciousness! The addition of the beef fry and caramelized onions is a fabulous surprise.

Beef Fry

1 Tbsp	olive oil
1 (6-oz) package	sliced beef fry, diced
1 medium	onion, diced

Burgers

3 lb	ground beef
¾ cup	seasoned panko crumbs
3 Tbsp	barbecue sauce
⅓	red onion, grated
2	egg yolks
¾ tsp	kosher salt
¼ tsp	black pepper

1. **Prepare the beef fry:** In a small frying pan over medium heat, heat olive oil. Add diced beef fry; toss until crispy, 4-6 minutes. Remove to a bowl. In the same frying pan, sauté diced onion over medium-high heat until golden, 8-10 minutes, stirring constantly. Remove from heat; combine with beef fry. Set aside.

2. **Prepare the burgers:** Line a baking sheet with parchment paper.

3. In a large bowl, combine ground beef, panko crumbs, barbecue sauce, grated onion, egg yolks, salt, and pepper. To form uniform patties, line the inside of a 4-inch jar lid with a small piece of plastic wrap. Press a small handful of ground beef mixture into the lid. Press down and level the mixture, then turn out onto prepared baking sheet.

4. Place 1 tablespoon beef fry/onion mixture onto the center of each patty. Fold the outer rim of the patty over the filling, pressing to close the opening. Place seam-side down on the baking sheet.

5. Coat grill with cooking spray; preheat grill. Grill patties for approximately 3 minutes, then flip and grill for approximately 3 minutes on the second side. Alternatively, grill on the stovetop in a grill pan coated with cooking spray or broil in a preheated oven on a grill pan coated with cooking spray. Cooking time remains the same.

6. Optional servings suggestions: Serve on pretzel buns or other buns of your choice, with Onion Marmalade (page 70), as pictured, or with Roasted Garlic Aioli Sauce (page 166)

—Variation

If you're short on time, you can mix the beef fry mixture into the meat mixture and then form the patties.

—Tips

These burgers freeze beautifully, filled or unfilled. They can be frozen raw after they're filled; defrost before grilling.

SWEET N' TANGY MEATBALLS

Meat **YIELDS** *6 servings*

THIS IS IT! No need to look further. This is the meatball recipe you will never retire.

Meatballs

2 lb	ground beef
1 cup	seasoned breadcrumbs
1	shallot, grated
2	eggs, lightly beaten
¼ cup	almond milk *or* soy milk
½ tsp	kosher salt
½ tsp	onion powder
½ tsp	garlic powder
⅛ tsp	black pepper

Sweet and Tangy Sauce

12 oz	chili sauce
12 oz	water (measure with the empty chili sauce bottle)
12 oz	apricot preserves
¼ cup	teriyaki sauce
2 Tbsp	dark brown sugar
2 Tbsp	rice vinegar
6 cloves	garlic, crushed

1. **Prepare the sweet and tangy sauce:** Combine sauce ingredients in a pot. Bring sauce to a boil over medium-high heat.

2. Meanwhile, in a large bowl, combine meatball ingredients. Mix by hand until well blended; do not overmix. Form into 1-inch balls. Drop meatballs into boiling sauce.

3. Cook for 30-45 minutes.

—Variation

To make in a crockpot: Coat a 4-6-quart slow cooker with cooking spray or line with a slow cooker liner. Preheat to high or low, depending on your time frame (see below). Whisk together sauce ingredients. Pour sauce into the slow cooker. In a large bowl, combine meatball ingredients. Form beef mixture into 1-inch balls; drop into sauce. Gently stir meatballs in the sauce to coat well. Cover slow cooker; cook for 2-2½ hours on high or 4-5 hours on low.

SIMPLY SAVORY LAMB CHOPS

Meat

YIELDS *4 servings (2 chops per serving)*

8	lamb chops

Marinade

4 cloves	garlic, crushed
1	shallot, finely diced
1 tsp	dried rosemary *or* **1 Tbsp** fresh rosemary (leaves only)
3 Tbsp	olive oil
¼ cup	red wine vinegar
1 Tbsp	kosher salt
½-1 tsp	black pepper

Perfect for that special occasion, these tender and succulent lamb chops are sure to impress.

1. **Prepare the marinade:** Combine all marinade ingredients in a large resealable bag. Shake well to combine.

2. Rinse and dry lamb chops. Add to marinade; seal bag. Marinate for 20-30 minutes at room temperature.

3. Pan sear, broil, or grill lamb chops for 2-3 minutes per side, or until desired doneness. Serve warm.

SMOKY BEEF RUB

Pareve **YIELDS** *2-2¼ cups*

Once you've tried this intensely flavor-packed spice blend, you will never go back to just salt and pepper to season your meat.

¾ cup	light brown sugar
¾ cup	turbinado sugar (see Note on page 44)
2 Tbsp	garlic powder
2 Tbsp	smoked paprika
2 Tbsp	instant coffee granules
2 Tbsp	cumin
½ Tbsp	dried rosemary
½ Tbsp	dried thyme
½ Tbsp	dried parsley flakes
½ Tbsp	dried basil

1. Combine spices well.

2. Use this rub as a primer for any meat that you will bake, grill, or roast. After meat has been spiced, simply bake, grill, or roast, or opt to add an additional sauce. Depending on the cut, follow the usual cooking directions for cooking time and covering.

3. If not using immediately, store rub or any leftover rub in an airtight container for up to 3 months.

SMOKY BARBECUED OVERNIGHT FLANKEN ROAST

Meat **YIELDS** *6 servings*

Overnight braising yields melt-in-your-mouth results. On short Fridays, I often roast this fabulous, foolproof flanken overnight for Shabbos lunch. Having special guests? This roast is an impressive alternative to an ordinary deli platter.

1 (3-lb)	flanken roast
1 tsp	chili powder
1 tsp	smoked paprika
½ tsp	garlic powder
¼ tsp	celery salt
⅛ tsp	black pepper
1 Tbsp	olive oil
¾ cup	ketchup
¾ cup	chili sauce
⅓ cup	dark brown sugar, packed
3 Tbsp	vinegar
3 Tbsp	fish-free Worcestershire sauce
1 tsp	liquid smoke
1 tsp	ground mustard
6 cloves	garlic, crushed

1. Preheat oven to 225°F. Set out a 9x13-inch baking pan.

2. Rinse roast; pat dry.

3. In a small bowl, combine chili powder, smoked paprika, garlic powder, celery salt, and pepper. Smear olive oil over the top of the roast; rub the spice mixture evenly over it.

4. Spray a grill pan with cooking spray; heat on stovetop over medium-high heat. Sear bottom of roast for 5 minutes. Turn roast over; sear spiced top for 5 minutes.

5. Transfer roast, bone-side down, to prepared baking pan.

6. In a small bowl, combine ketchup, chili sauce, brown sugar, vinegar, Worcestershire sauce, liquid smoke, mustard, and garlic. Pour mixture over roast. Seal tightly with foil, then wrap the entire pan with foil and place on oven's center rack. Bake for 10-12 hours.

7. Let rest for 10 minutes before slicing. Best served warm.

— Variation

Instead of overnight-baking, after searing meat, preheat oven to 325°F; roast for 3½-4 hours.

CHILI-LIME RUBBED DELMONICO

Meat **YIELDS** *6-10 servings*

1 (3-5 lb) Delmonico roast
1 Tbsp olive oil
• honey, for drizzling

Chili-Lime Rub

1 Tbsp lime juice
1 Tbsp chili powder
1 tsp coriander
¼-½ tsp black pepper
2 tsp kosher salt

This is an easy, elegant way to prepare beef that is tender and juicy. The chili-lime rub provides a sweet heat flavor that pleases all palates.

1. **Prepare the chili-lime rub:** In a small bowl, combine rub ingredients to form a paste.

2. Rinse meat; pat dry. Smear meat with olive oil. Smear chili-lime rub all over roast. Marinate roast for at least 20-30 minutes or overnight in the refrigerator.

3. Allow roast to come to room temperature for 20 minutes.

4. Preheat oven to 325°F. Set out a 9x13-inch pan. Spray a large skillet with cooking spray; heat pan over medium-high heat. Sear meat for 10 minutes on each side.

5. Transfer meat to prepared pan; drizzle with honey. Bake, uncovered, until internal temperature reaches 130°F for medium rare (approximately 35-40 minutes for a 3-pound roast; 45-60 minutes for a 5-pound roast).

6. Let rest for 10 minutes before slicing.

— **Note** —
A meat thermometer is a great tool to help monitor meat doneness.

Meat

AROMATIC VEAL BREAST

Meat   **YIELDS** *6-10 servings*

Tender, melt-in-your-mouth veal is a show-stopping main for your Yom Tov or Shabbos feast. This impressive dish can be assembled with minimal hands-on time. The intense flavor of the porcini and herb rub, coupled with the braising liquid, is outstanding.

1 (3-5-lb) veal roast *or* veal breast with pocket

1-2 Tbsp olive oil, for smearing

Rub

4 cloves garlic, crushed

1 tsp dried rosemary

1 tsp dried thyme

1 oz dried porcini mushrooms

1 tsp kosher salt

¼ tsp black pepper

Braising Liquid

¾ cup chicken broth *or* **¾ cup** water + **¾ tsp** consommé powder

¼ cup dry white wine

3 Tbsp ketchup *or* barbecue sauce

3 Tbsp apricot jam

2 Tbsp honey

1 Tbsp yellow mustard

2 tsp balsamic vinegar

1. Preheat oven to 350°F. Prepare a 9x13-inch baking pan.

2. Place all rub ingredients into a food processor; pulse to combine.

3. Rinse meat; pat dry. Place meat, bone-side down, into prepared pan. Smear roast with olive oil; spread rub all over roast.

4. Combine all braising liquid ingredients in a medium bowl; whisk until smooth. Pour liquid around the roast. Cover pan with foil; bake for 1½ hours.

5. Remove from oven. Baste roast with braising liquid. Return to oven; bake for additional 1-1½ hours, basting every 30 minutes, until meat is tender. Roast can be uncovered for the last 30 minutes so that a crust forms.

6. Let rest for 10 minutes before slicing. Serve warm.

—**Tip**—
Veal pocket can be stuffed with your favorite stuffing, if desired.

BRAISED BBQ RACK OF RIBS

Meat

YIELDS *5-6 servings (2 ribs per serving)*

BBQ Sauce

1 Tbsp	olive oil
1 medium	onion, diced
2 cloves	garlic, crushed
1	jalapeño pepper, seeded and diced
1 (6-oz) can	tomato paste
¾ cup	apple cider vinegar
½ cup	chili sauce
½ cup	dark brown sugar
1 Tbsp	molasses
1 Tbsp	fish-free Worcestershire sauce
1 tsp	liquid smoke

Spice Rub

3 Tbsp	light brown sugar
2 Tbsp	chili powder
2 Tbsp	kosher salt
1 Tbsp	paprika
1 Tbsp	smoked paprika
1 Tbsp	onion powder
1 Tbsp	garlic powder
1 Tbsp	ground mustard
1 Tbsp	black pepper

Ribs

2 (2½-3 lb) racks	ribs (5-6 ribs per rack)
½ cup	Dijon mustard
½ cup	apple juice

These ribs offer classic BBQ flavor, but are made simply in the oven. Wrapping the ribs in foil helps keep them moist throughout the low and slow cook time, while broiling at the end gives them a deliciously crispy crust.

1. **Prepare the BBQ sauce:** Heat oil in a medium saucepan over medium-high heat. Add onion, garlic, and jalapeño. Cook for 8 minutes, stirring often, until mixture begins to brown lightly. Stir in remaining sauce ingredients. Bring mixture to a boil; reduce heat to medium-low. Allow mixture to simmer for 20-30 minutes as the mixture thickens. Stir occasionally to prevent sauce from burning. Remove from heat. Cool; refrigerate until ready to use. (The sauce can be made in advance and refrigerated. It's so good that I double it and use on any meat dish — just saying.)

2. **Prepare the spice rub:** Combine spice rub ingredients in a small bowl; set aside.

3. **Prepare the ribs:** Space oven racks evenly in oven. Preheat oven to 325°F. Set out 2 roasting pans.

4. Rinse each rack of ribs; pat dry. Lay each rack on a large piece of foil. Smear 2 tablespoons Dijon mustard over each rack. Sprinkle each rack with spice rub, patting to coat well. Fold foil upward to create a boat-like shape. Drizzle ¼ cup apple juice over each rack. Seal the foil; transfer each wrapped rack to a prepared pan. Cover pans tightly with foil. Place pans in the oven, one roasting pan on each rack. Bake for 3½-4 hours, until fork tender (you can tell doneness by unwrapping the foil and using a pair of tongs or a fork pierced between the first two bones to lift by one end; if it bends easily, it's ready. Alternatively, you can unwrap the pan and see if the meat pulls easily with a fork). Halfway through baking, rotate pans on the oven racks so that they bake evenly.

5. Remove pans from the oven. Open foil covers. Raise oven heat to broil. Slather ribs with sauce. Broil one rack of ribs at a time on lowest oven rack for 5-10 minutes until meat begins to char slightly.

6. Allow meat to rest for 10 minutes before slicing apart ribs.

— Tip —

This recipe works great with spare ribs, and it's freezer friendly, too!

GARLIC-CRUSTED BRISKET

Meat **YIELDS** *6-10 servings*

This is not your typical traditional recipe. The combination of roasted and sautéed garlic creates a sweet and savory explosion of flavor. I am sure that this buttery soft brisket will become your new classic.

1 (3-5-lb)	first cut brisket
•	kosher salt, for sprinkling
•	black pepper, for sprinkling
2 Tbsp	olive oil
1 large	onion, diced
16 cloves	garlic, peeled and finely chopped
½ tsp	dried thyme
1 cup	chicken broth, *or* **1 cup** water + **1 tsp** consommé powder
¾ cup	dry white wine
2 Tbsp	red wine vinegar
2	bay leaves

Roasted Garlic

1 head	garlic
1 Tbsp	olive oil
•	kosher salt, to taste
•	black pepper, to taste
1 slice	lemon

1. **Prepare the roasted garlic:** Preheat oven to 350°F. Set out a small baking sheet.

2. Slice off top of the garlic head, exposing all the cloves; place onto the center of a piece of foil large enough to enclose garlic. Drizzle with olive oil. Sprinkle with salt and pepper. Place lemon slice on garlic head. Seal foil; place on prepared baking sheet or another piece of foil. Bake for 45 minutes, until garlic becomes golden and fragrant. Remove from oven; cool. This can be prepared in advance and refrigerated until ready for use.

3. **Prepare the garlic-crusted brisket:** Preheat oven to 325°F. Set out a 9x13-inch baking pan.

4. Rinse meat; pat dry. Lightly season with kosher salt and black pepper. Place meat into prepared pan; set aside.

5. In a skillet, heat olive oil medium heat. Add onion; sauté for 8-10 minutes. Add garlic and thyme. Stir constantly for 2 minutes until fragrant. Gradually add chicken broth, wine, vinegar, and bay leaves, stirring to combine. Bring mixture to a boil. Reduce heat; simmer for 5 minutes to form a sauce.

6. While the mixture simmers, squeeze the roasted garlic cloves out of the head by pressing them up from the bottom into a small bowl; mash with a fork until a paste forms. Spread the garlic paste over the brisket.

7. Pour the sautéed onion/garlic sauce over roast. Cover; seal baking pan with foil. Bake 2⅓-3 hours, or until roast is fork tender. Remove and discard bay leaves. Cool; slice meat against the grain. Transfer to a serving platter. To serve, pour warmed sauce over meat.

BEST-EVER STICKY RIBS

Meat **YIELDS** *6 servings*

One bite is all the proof you need that these are indeed the best sticky ribs ever!

3-5 lbs.	English ribs (see Note)
1 tsp	chili powder
½ tsp	garlic powder
¼ tsp	onion powder
⅛ tsp	black pepper

Sticky Sauce

1 cup	beef broth *or* **1 cup** water + **1 Tbsp** beef consommé powder
1 cup	barbecue sauce
½ cup	hoisin sauce
⅓ cup	honey
2 Tbsp	rice vinegar
2 Tbsp	fish-free Worcestershire sauce
2 Tbsp	prepared horseradish
1 tsp	ground mustard
3 cloves	garlic, crushed

1. Preheat oven to 325°F. Set out a 9x13-inch baking pan.

2. In a small bowl, stir together chili powder, garlic powder, onion powder, and pepper. Coat each rib with this rub. Place ribs into prepared baking pan.

3. **Prepare the sticky sauce:** Combine all sauce ingredients.

4. Place ribs into prepared pan; pour sauce over ribs. Seal pan tightly with foil. Place in oven; bake for 3 hours or until tender.

— Note —————

English ribs are cut parallel to the bone, and are generally a larger portion, so you can count on 1 rib per person. These ribs tend to hold their shape even after braising, which ultimately results in an impressive presentation.

EDIE'S FRENCH ROAST

Meat **YIELDS** *6-10 servings*

1 (3-5-lb)	french roast
2	onions, diced
4 cloves	garlic, crushed
2 Tbsp	canola oil
¼ cup	vinegar
½ cup	water
¾ cup	dark brown sugar
½ cup	ketchup
1 tsp	cornstarch
•	kosher salt, for sprinkling
•	black pepper, for sprinkling

Ever since I was a child, my Aunt Edie's classic roast recipe has been an all-time favorite in my extended family. Its popularity when I posted it online proves that anything old can be new again. I'm so happy to share this with you.

1. Preheat oven to 325°F. Set out a 9x13-inch roasting pan.

2. Heat oil in a skillet over medium heat. Add onions and garlic; sauté for about 20 minutes.

3. Meanwhile, in a small saucepan, whisk together vinegar, water, sugar, ketchup, and cornstarch. Bring mixture to a boil over medium-high heat; cook until thickened. Remove from heat; set aside.

4. Sprinkle roast with salt and pepper. Pour sautéed onion/garlic mixture over roast. Bake, uncovered, for 30 minutes.

5. Pour thickened sauce over roast; return to oven. Bake, uncovered, until desired doneness. After 30 minutes begin checking for doneness. Test roast with meat thermometer; internal temperature should be 130°F for medium rare.

6. Let rest for 10 minutes before slicing. Best served warm with its sauce.

Sides

ROASTED VEGGIE PLATTER

Pareve **YIELDS** *6-8 servings*

Roasted veggies seem to be a no-brainer, but after multiple requests to share this recipe, I decided to include it in my cookbook.

Roasted Peppers

1 (16-oz) bag	mini tri-colored peppers, halved and seeded
2 Tbsp	olive oil
1 tsp	kosher salt
¼-½ tsp	black pepper
1 Tbsp	rice vinegar

Roasted Mushrooms

6	Portobello mushroom caps, cut into ¼-inch slices (5-6 slices per cap)
2 Tbsp	olive oil
1 tsp	kosher salt
¼-½ tsp	black pepper
1-2 Tbsp	teriyaki sauce
2 tsp	honey

Roasted Zucchini

4 large	zucchinis, peel on, sliced ¼-inch thick on an angle
2-3 Tbsp	olive oil
1 tsp	kosher salt
¼-½ tsp	black pepper
1 Tbsp	balsamic vinegar

1. **Roast the peppers:** Preheat oven to 450°F. Prepare a baking sheet, with or without parchment paper. In a medium bowl, combine oil, salt, pepper, and rice vinegar. Toss peppers in mixture; transfer peppers to prepared baking sheet. Roast for 30-40 minutes, tossing peppers halfway through roasting time.

2. **Roast the mushrooms:** Lower oven temperature to 400°F. Prepare a baking sheet, with or without parchment paper. In a medium bowl, combine oil, salt, pepper, and teriyaki sauce. Toss mushrooms in mixture; transfer to prepared baking sheet. Drizzle with honey. Roast for 25-30 minutes, tossing mushrooms halfway through the roasting time.

3. **Roast the zucchini:** Maintain oven temperature at 400°F. Prepare a baking sheet, with or without parchment paper. In a medium bowl, combine oil, salt, pepper, and balsamic vinegar. Toss zucchinis in mixture; transfer to prepared baking sheet. Roast for 25-30 minutes, tossing zucchinis halfway through the roasting. Zucchinis can be roasted at the same time as the mushrooms.

4. Arrange vegetables on a platter. Serve immediately.

5. If not serving right away, store vegetables separately.

Tip

If not serving right away, roasted vegetables are best when just brought to room temperature. If you want to reheat them, heat them, uncovered, in a 200°F oven or over the inverted top of a slow cooker.

ZUCCHINI SPEARS WITH CREAMY LEMON-BASIL DIPPING SAUCE

Pareve   YIELDS *8 servings*

A no-fuss vegetable side or perfect party food. Make sure to double the recipe, as these have a tendency to disappear.

4 medium   zucchinis

¼-⅓ cup   seasoned panko crumbs

Creamy Lemon-Basil Sauce

½ cup   mayonnaise

¼ cup   freshly squeezed lemon juice

¼ cup   fresh basil leaves

2 Tbsp   extra virgin olive oil

1 tsp   honey

½ tsp   kosher salt

½ tsp   lemon zest

¼ tsp   black pepper

1. Slice ¼-inch from the top of each zucchini. Do not peel them. Rinse; pat dry. Slice each zucchini in half lengthwise, then widthwise. Slice each quarter into thirds to form spears. Place spears into a large bowl.

2. Preheat oven to broil. Line a baking sheet with parchment paper; lightly coat with cooking spray.

3. **Prepare the creamy lemon-basil sauce:** Place all sauce ingredients into a tall container; use an immersion blender to combine. Alternatively, use a food processor fitted with the "S" blade to combine all sauce ingredients.

4. Pour half the dressing over the zucchini spears; toss to coat. Place each spear on prepared baking sheet; sprinkle with panko crumbs.

5. Broil on center rack for 15 minutes.

6. Serve with remaining sauce.

TERIYAKI GREEN BEANS

Pareve **YIELDS** *6-8 servings*

1½-2 lb	green beans
3 cubes	frozen sautéed onions, defrosted (see Note)
¼ cup	teriyaki sauce
1½ Tbsp	honey
1 tsp	garlic salt, *or* **½ tsp** kosher salt + **½ tsp** garlic powder
¼ tsp	black pepper

One Friday night, I realized that I had blanched the green beans but had no dressing. My daughter whipped up a quick hack that she thought of on the spot. By the end of the meal, there wasn't one green bean left. Clearly, necessity IS the mother of invention.

1. Bring a 6-quart pot of water to a rolling boil. Add green beans; blanch for 3 minutes. Immediately transfer green beans to a strainer and run cold water over them to stop the cooking process.

2. Combine onions, teriyaki sauce, honey, garlic salt, and pepper.

3. Toss green beans with teriyaki mixture before serving. Serve at room temperature.

— Note —

To caramelize your own onions, simply heat 1 tablespoon olive oil in a saucepan and sauté a small diced onion over low heat until caramelized, about 30 minutes. Raise heat for the last 1½ minutes, stirring constantly.

SPANISH RICED CAULIFLOWER

Pareve **YIELDS** *6 servings*

A new, healthy twist on a superb classic. .

1 (14-16 oz) bag	riced cauliflower, fresh or frozen, defrosted
2 Tbsp	olive oil
1 small	onion, finely diced
1	leek (white part only), finely diced
3 cloves	garlic, crushed
1½ cups	marinara sauce
3 Tbsp	ketchup
1 tsp	kosher salt
¼-½ tsp	black pepper
¼ tsp	onion powder
¼ tsp	garlic powder
½ tsp	dried oregano

1. In a large frying pan over medium heat, heat oil. Add onion and leek; sauté until translucent, 3-5 minutes. Add garlic; sauté 2-3 minutes. Add cauliflower; sauté for 2 minutes. Add marinara sauce, ketchup, and spices. Stir well.

2. Cover pan; cook 5 minutes. Remove cover; stir well. Raise heat; stir until all liquid is absorbed.

— Note —

To make your own cauliflower rice: If using frozen cauliflower, defrost slightly before processing. Place cauliflower florets into a food processor fitted with the "S" blade. (You may need to process it in 2 or 3 batches.) Pulse 2-3 times until a rice-like consistency forms. Set aside.

LEMONY-GARLIC BROCCOLI

Pareve **YIELDS** *6 servings*

I like to prepare healthy, well-balanced meals for my family. This broccoli tops their all-time request list.

1 (32-oz) bag	frozen *or* fresh broccoli florets
1 tsp	table salt
3 Tbsp	extra light olive oil
5 cloves	garlic, peeled and sliced
3 slices	lemon, cut into tiny wedges
1 Tbsp	kosher salt
¼ tsp	black pepper
¼ tsp	garlic powder

1. Fill an 8-quart pot halfway with water; add table salt. Bring to a rolling boil over high heat. Add broccoli; cover. Boil for 3-4 minutes. Drain broccoli; rinse under cold water to halt cooking process. Set aside.

2. In a large skillet, heat olive oil over medium heat. Add garlic slices; stir well for about 30 seconds to make garlic-infused fragrant oil. Add broccoli and lemon wedges; toss together. Season with salt, pepper, and garlic powder. Toss together over high heat for about 1 minute. Promptly transfer to a serving dish; serve hot.

ZUCCHINI SPINACH BALLS

Pareve

YIELDS *5-6 servings (16 balls)*

1 Tbsp	olive oil
1 medium	onion, diced
12 oz	frozen chopped spinach, thawed and drained
2 medium	zucchinis, peeled and shredded (place in paper towel and wring out all moisture)
2 cloves	garlic, crushed
½ cup	seasoned breadcrumbs *or* panko crumbs
½-1 tsp	lemon zest
2 Tbsp	lemon juice
½ tsp	sea salt
⅛ tsp	black pepper
1	egg

Tomato Sauce

1 Tbsp	olive oil
1 medium	onion, diced
½ tsp	sea salt
⅛ tsp	black pepper
2 cloves	garlic, crushed
½ tsp	dried basil
1 (8-oz)	can tomato sauce
½ cup	tomato soup *or* **½ cup** hot water + **1 tsp** tomato soup powder
1 cup	marinara sauce

A creative and fun way to balance your family's meals and give them greens that they'll really enjoy.

1. Line a baking sheet with parchment paper.

2. In a medium sauté pan over medium heat, heat olive oil. Add onion; sauté for 5 minutes, or until translucent. Add spinach, zucchinis, and garlic. Cover pan; cook for 2 minutes. Remove cover; cook 2 minutes until all liquid is absorbed and mixture is dry. Remove from heat.

3. Add breadcrumbs, lemon zest, lemon juice, salt, pepper, and egg. Mix well until combined. With gloved hands, shape mixture into golf ball-size balls. Place balls on prepared baking sheet; refrigerate for 15 minutes.

4. **Prepare the sauce:** In a large skillet over medium heat, heat oil. Add onion, sauté for 5 minutes. Stir in salt, pepper, garlic, and basil. Add tomato sauce, tomato soup, and marinara sauce; bring to a boil. Cover skillet; simmer for 5 minutes.

5. Gently lower zucchini-spinach balls into the sauce. Cover; simmer for 30 minutes.

-Tip-

Do not stir the balls while cooking. Rather, gently shake the pot to allow the balls to set properly.

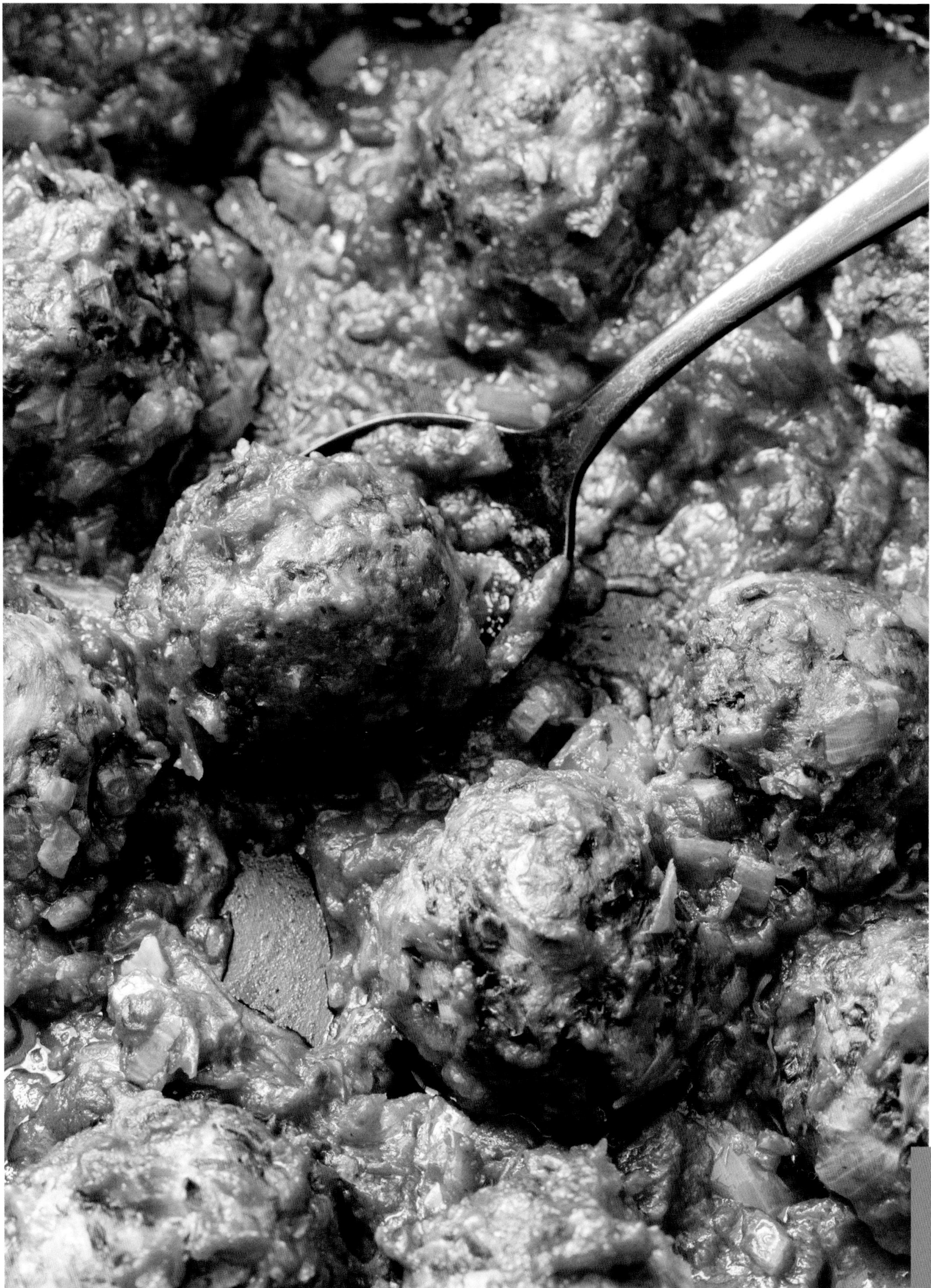

MUSHROOM LEEK TARTLETS

Pareve

YIELDS *14 mini tarts or 1 (9-inch) round*

14	frozen mini tart shells *or* **1 (9-inch)** frozen pie shell
3 Tbsp	olive oil
3	shallots, sliced
2	leeks, white and light green parts only, diced
1 clove	garlic, crushed
7 oz	shiitake *or* baby bella mushrooms, sliced (about 3 cups)
1 Tbsp	teriyaki sauce
¼ cup	white wine
1 tsp	sea salt
¼-½ tsp	black pepper
4	eggs, slightly beaten with a fork

I am usually not one to prepare in advance and freeze. However, these savory tartlets come together quickly, pair with any dish, and freeze like a dream.

1. Preheat oven to 350°F. Set out a baking sheet.

2. Place tart shells or pie shell on prepared baking sheet. Prebake tart shells for 7 minutes or 9-inch round for 10 minutes; set aside.

3. Heat oil in a medium skillet over medium heat. Add shallots, leeks, and garlic; sauté for 5-8 minutes. Add mushrooms; cook for 5 minutes, stirring often.

4. Add teriyaki sauce, wine, salt, and pepper. Cook until wine reduces, 3-5 minutes.

5. Remove skillet from heat. Cool mixture slightly. Add eggs. Mix well. Divide mixture evenly between tart shells or pour into pie shell.

6. Bake 20-30 minutes for mini tarts or45-60 minutes for 9-inch round, until tops puff slightly and turn golden.

BRUSSELS SPROUTS FRITTERS

Pareve **YIELDS** *16 fritters*

These fritters are a fun way to get your finicky eaters to enjoy their greens.

Fritters

½ cup	seasoned breadcrumbs *or* panko crumbs
½ cup	flour
1 tsp	baking powder
2 tsp	kosher salt, divided
½ cup	nondairy milk
1	egg
2 cups	thinly sliced Brussels sprouts
½ cup	finely chopped Vidalia onion
½ tsp	black pepper
4 cups	canola oil, for frying

Sirachanaise

2 tsp	lemon juice
1 tsp	Dijon mustard
¾ tsp	kosher salt
2 Tbsp	mayonnaise
¾ cup	canola oil
1½ tsp	sriracha
1 clove	garlic, crushed

1. **Prepare the srirachanaise:** In a medium bowl, whisk together lemon juice, mustard, salt, and mayonnaise until smooth. Slowly drizzle in oil, whisking constantly until the mixture thickens. Whisk in sriracha and garlic. Cover bowl; chill.

2. **Prepare the fritters:** In a large bowl, stir together breadcrumbs, flour, baking powder, and 1 teaspoon salt. In a small bowl, whisk together nondairy milk and egg. Pour milk/egg mixture into crumb mixture; stir until combined.

3. Toss Brussels sprouts with onion, pepper, and ½ teaspoon salt. Fold into crumb mixture.

4. In a large skillet, heat oil over medium heat. Drop batter by the tablespoon into hot oil. Be sure not to overcrowd the pan. Cook until golden, about 6 minutes. Turn and cook second side until golden, about 4 minutes. Remove fritters; drain on paper towels.

5. Sprinkle fritters with remaining ½ teaspoon salt. Serve with srirachanaise.

La Gazzetta
IL RAPPORTO
Mosca più car
tredicesim
IL PREMIER
La gioia del numero 10
AUDISIO NELLO SPORT

ROASTED ACORN SQUASH WITH LEMON MAPLE DRESSING

Pareve   **YIELDS** *8 servings*

The vibrant colors of this dish remind me of the changing colors of fall foliage. Adding a burst of color and flavor, the combination of squash and cranberries really adds a wow factor to your plate.

3 small acorn squash, peel on, sliced

1 Vidalia onion, sliced

3 Tbsp olive oil

1 tsp kosher salt

½ tsp black pepper

1 cup fresh *or* frozen cranberries

Lemon Maple Dressing

¼ cup olive oil

2 Tbsp lemon juice

2 Tbsp pure maple syrup

1 tsp Dijon mustard

• sea salt, to taste

• black pepper, to taste

1. Preheat oven to 450°F. Set out a baking sheet.

2. Spread acorn squash and onion on prepared pan. Drizzle with olive oil, salt, and pepper. Toss to coat. Roast for 30 minutes.

3. Remove from oven. Toss again; turn over large pieces. Toss with cranberries. Roast for 15 minutes.

4. Remove from oven; cool.

5. **Prepare the dressing:** Combine dressing ingredients in a small bowl.

6. When ready to serve, pour dressing over roasted vegetables. Toss; serve warm or at room temperature.

— Note —

If you are reheating the vegetables, reheat, uncovered, over indirect heat (e.g., a hotplate, inverted cover of slow cooker, warming drawer) or in a 200°F oven.

— Variation —

Acorn squash can be substituted with butternut squash or sweet potato.

HONEY MUSTARD POTATOES

Pareve **YIELDS** *10 servings*

An all-around, any time, any place, crowd pleaser.

2 lb pebble (mini) potatoes
⅓ cup yellow mustard
½ cup honey
3 Tbsp onion soup mix

1. Preheat oven to 400°F. Coat a 9x13-inch baking pan with cooking spray.

2. Rinse potatoes; place potatoes into a medium pot. Cover with water; bring to a boil. Boil for 10 minutes; drain. (This step ensures that potatoes are completely baked.)

3. Place potatoes in a single layer in prepared baking pan. In a small bowl or measuring cup, combine mustard, honey, and onion soup mix; drizzle over potatoes. Toss to coat.

4. Bake, uncovered, for 55-60 minutes, tossing occasionally. Serve warm.

Tip

If time does not permit boiling the potatoes in Step 2, simply begin with Step 3. Fork-test potatoes after baking time to be sure they are baked through.

CANDIED BEEF FRY AND POTATOES AU GRATIN

Meat YIELDS *12 servings*

Serve these great tasting scalloped potatoes as a satisfying side. It's an easy, hearty dish that feeds a crowd, is budget-friendly, and will leave everyone asking for seconds.

Candied Beef Fry

2 (6-8-oz) packages	beef fry
¼ cup	brown sugar
2 Tbsp	pure maple syrup
⅛-¼ tsp	black pepper

Caramelized Onions

4 large	Spanish onions, halved, sliced into ¼-inch slices
3 Tbsp	olive oil
1 tsp	kosher salt
½ tsp	black pepper

Potatoes

2 lb.-	red potatoes (about 6), peeled and sliced into ¼-inch rounds
3 Tbsp	olive oil
4 cloves	garlic, crushed
1 Tbsp	soy sauce
1 Tbsp	red wine vinegar
1 tsp	dried rosemary
1 tsp	dried basil
1 tsp	dried parsley flakes
1 Tbsp	kosher salt
¼ tsp	black pepper

Tip

This dish can be prepared in advance and refrigerated; it tastes even better the second time around (although I can't imagine you'll have leftovers).

1. Preheat oven to 350°F. Line a baking sheet with parchment paper. Coat a 9x13-inch oven-to-table casserole dish with cooking spray; set aside.

2. **Prepare the candied beef fry:** In a small bowl, combine sugar, maple syrup, and pepper.

3. Place beef fry slices on prepared baking sheet. Cut 4 slices into ½-inch pieces (for garnish). Brush both sides of beef fry with half of the brown sugar mixture. Bake for 10 minutes.

4. Remove from oven; turn slices over. Brush with remaining brown sugar mixture. Bake 10-15 minutes until beef fry is caramelized and somewhat crispy. Set aside to cool. If desired, chop the ½-inch pieces into a smaller crumble for garnish. Beef fry is easier to cut while warm.

5. **Prepare the caramelized onions:** In a skillet over medium heat, heat olive oil. Add onions, salt, and pepper; sauté for at least 20-30 minutes, until onions have softened. Raise heat; slightly caramelize (brown) the onion, stirring constantly, for about 3 minutes. Remove from heat.

6. **Prepare the potatoes:** In a large bowl, combine potatoes, olive oil, garlic, soy sauce, vinegar, herbs, and spices. Toss to coat potatoes.

7. **Assemble the au gratin:** Place a thin layer of caramelized onions into prepared casserole dish, to just cover the bottom. Layer half the potatoes in 3 slightly overlapping rows. Reserve ½ cup caramelized onions. Spread remaining caramelized onions over potato layer. Arrange candied beef fry slices over onions.

8. Layer remaining potatoes in 3 slightly overlapping rows over onions. Sprinkle with reserved caramelized onions and chopped beef fry.

9. Cover casserole dish with foil. Bake for 1 hour 15 minutes. Remove from oven; check that potatoes are soft. Add additional bake time if necessary.

10. Uncover; bake additional 10-15 minutes.

SWEET POTATO STACKS

Pareve **YIELDS** *12 stacks*

Easy and convenient, these individual stacks can be dressed up or dressed down, and they are always downright delicious.

2 medium	sweet potatoes
2 medium	Japanese yams (see Note)
1 Tbsp	canola oil
2 Tbsp	dark brown sugar
2 Tbsp	silan *or* pure maple syrup
2 Tbsp	lemon juice
⅛ tsp	cayenne pepper
½ tsp	cinnamon

1. Preheat oven to 375°F. Coat 12 muffin cups with cooking spray.

2. Peel sweet potatoes and yams; slice into ¼-inch rounds. Transfer to a large bowl.

3. In a small bowl, combine oil, brown sugar, silan, lemon juice, cayenne pepper, and cinnamon. Pour half the dressing over potato rounds; toss to coat well. Place a sweet potato round into each muffin cup. Place a Japanese yam round on the sweet potato. Repeat once for a total of 4 rounds per stack, alternating between yam and sweet potato. Brush the top of each stack with dressing. Seal muffin tin with foil. Bake for 30-40 minutes, until potatoes are tender.

4. Remove from oven; discard foil. Drizzle remaining dressing evenly over the potatoes. Allow stacks to cool. Gently lift stacks out of the cups.

Notes

Japanese yams are a readily available variety of sweet potato. If you cannot find them, use 4 sweet potatoes.

You can choose to make your stacks higher with more rounds per stack. Adjust the cook time, as it will take longer for the potatoes to cook all the way through.

Tip

Buy sweet potatoes and yams that are similar in size to yield visually appealing, even stacks.

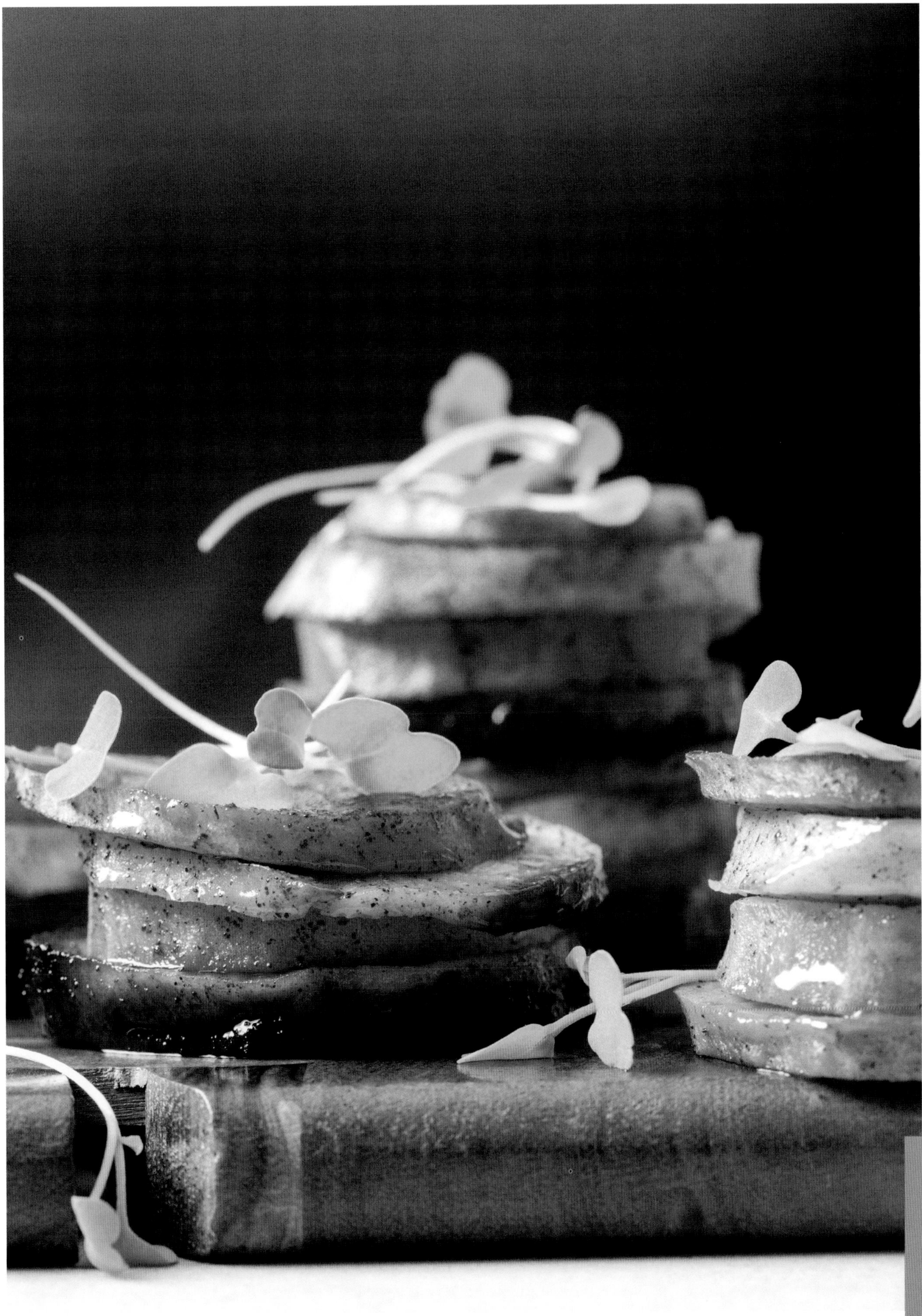

APPLE GALETTE

Pareve   YIELDS *8 servings*

Simple preparation with a beautiful presentation. This sensational side can also double as delicious dessert.

Dough

1 cup	flour
2 tsp	sugar
¼ tsp	sea salt
6 Tbsp	margarine, cold, cut into small pieces
2 Tbsp	ice water

Apple Filling

3	apples, peeled and sliced (1 Granny Smith and 2 firm Pink Lady *or* Gala)
2 Tbsp	sugar
½ tsp	cinnamon
1 Tbsp	vanilla sugar
1 tsp	lemon juice
2 Tbsp	raspberry jam

Topping

⅓ cup	ground almonds
4 tsp	turbinado sugar (see Note on page 44), **plus** more for sprinkling

1. **Prepare the dough:** In a large bowl, combine flour, sugar, salt, and margarine by hand. Mix until fine crumbs form. Add ice water; knead until a dough forms. Shape dough into a ball; wrap in plastic wrap. Refrigerate for 30 minutes.

2. Preheat oven to 375°F. Prepare a baking sheet.

3. **Prepare the apples:** In a medium bowl, toss apple slices with sugar, cinnamon, vanilla sugar, and lemon juice. Set aside.

4. Remove prepared dough from the refrigerator. Lightly flour a sheet of parchment paper. Place dough in center of paper; flatten to a disc. Top with a second sheet of parchment paper. Roll out to a 12-inch circle. Remove and discard top parchment sheet. Transfer dough with parchment onto prepared baking sheet.

5. Melt raspberry jam in a microwave-safe bowl in the microwave for 30 seconds. Leaving a 2-inch border, brush jam onto the dough. Lay coated apple slices over jam, starting at the edge of the jam. Working your way inward, lay apples side by side, overlapping the inner slices slightly over the outer circle's apples. Work inward until all slices are used.

6. **Prepare the topping:** Combine topping ingredients. Sprinkle topping over the apples.

7. Using the parchment paper as a guide, gently fold the border dough over the apples, pleating as needed and pressing down lightly to secure the dough over the fruit.

8. Brush the crust with water; sprinkle with turbinado sugar.

9. Bake for 50-55 minutes or until golden.

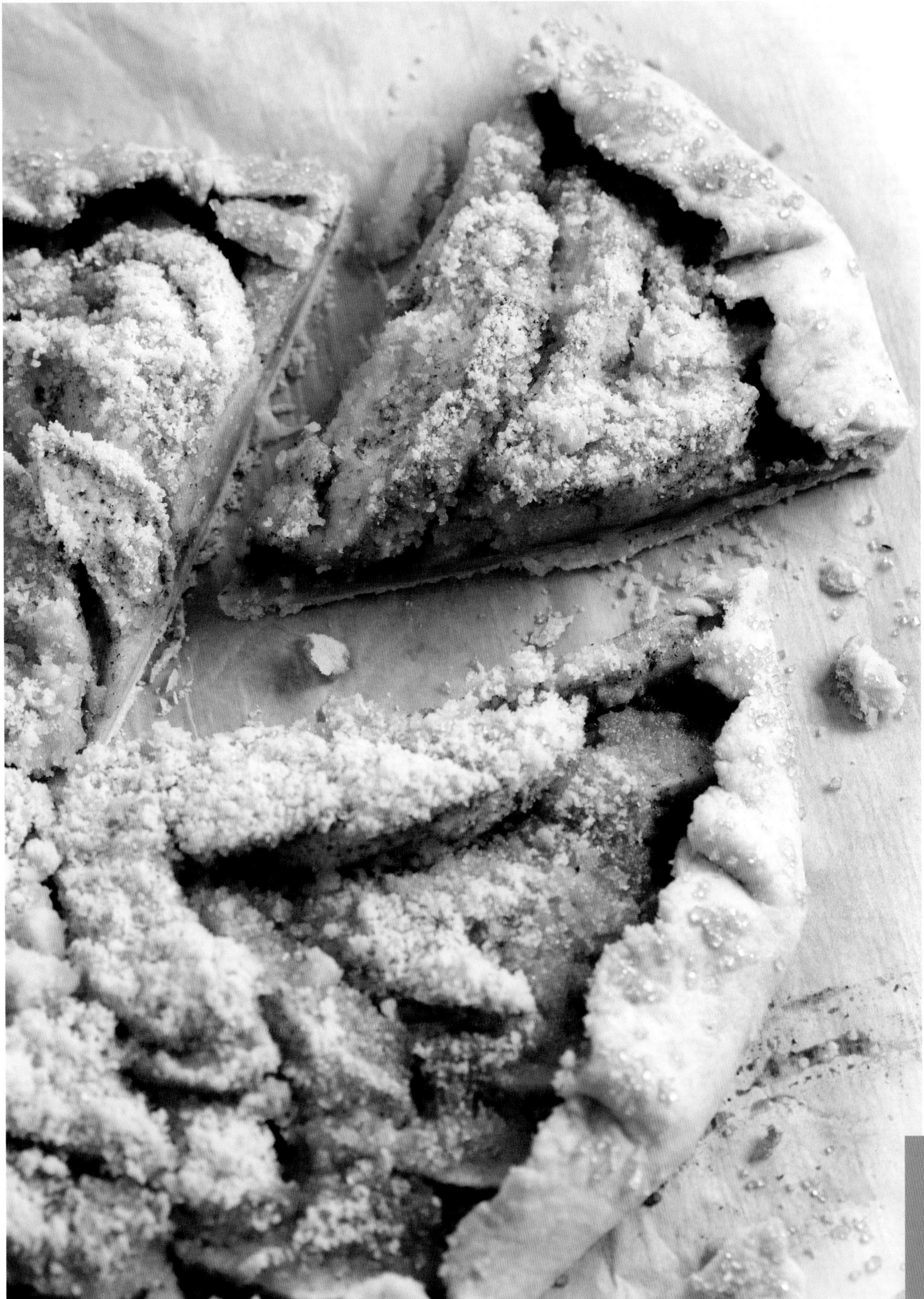

STRAWBERRY, RHUBARB, AND PEAR COBBLER

Pareve   YIELDS *8 servings*

What's not to like about a fabulous fruit cobbler? The perfect balance of tart and sweet makes this a great side dish.

8 oz	frozen strawberries (about 1½ cups)
8 oz	frozen rhubarb (about 1½ cups)
½ cup	sugar + **2 Tbsp** sugar, divided
1 tsp	rum *or* lemon juice
2 Tbsp	cornstarch
3	Bartlett pears, peeled and diced
1½ cups	old-fashioned oats
1¼ cups	flour
⅓ cup	almond flour *or* ground almonds
¾ cup	light brown sugar
½ tsp	baking powder
½ tsp	kosher salt
½ tsp	cinnamon
½ cup	canola oil
1 Tbsp	vanilla extract

1. In a large pot, combine strawberries and rhubarb with ½ cup sugar. Heat over medium heat, stirring occasionally, for about 15 minutes until fruit becomes tender and juices are released. Add rum.

2. Combine cornstarch and remaining 2 tablespoons sugar in a small bowl; whisk into fruit mixture. Cook, stirring continuously, until mixture thickens. Remove pot from heat; cool.

3. When fruit mixture is cooled, stir in diced pears.

4. Preheat oven to 350°F. Coat a 9x13-inch baking pan or 10-inch round pan with cooking spray.

5. Combine oats, flour, almond flour, brown sugar, baking powder, salt, and cinnamon. Add oil and vanilla extract. Stir until crumbs form and mixture becomes streusel-like.

6. Press ⅔ of the crumbs into the pan in an even layer. Spread fruit mixture over crumbs. Sprinkle with remaining crumbs.

7. Bake for 50-55 minutes, until crumbs are golden brown.

ROASTED VEGGIES AND QUINOA

Pareve   YIELDS 6 servings

Quinoa

1 cup	quinoa
2 cups	broth *or* **2 cups** water + **1 packet** Lipton Ranch for Soup and Dip Mix

Roasted Vegetables

1	red bell pepper
1	yellow bell pepper
2	zucchinis, halved lengthwise
1	eggplant, halved lengthwise
1	red onion, cut into ½-inch rounds
3 Tbsp	olive oil
1 Tbsp	kosher salt
½ tsp	black pepper

Dressing

2 cloves	garlic, crushed
⅓ cup	olive oil
2 Tbsp	lemon juice
2 Tbsp	pure maple syrup
2 tsp	Dijon mustard
1 tsp	dark brown sugar
1 tsp	dried basil
1 tsp	dried parsley flakes
½ tsp	kosher salt
¼ tsp	black pepper

My family and I have been quinoa fans for quite some time. I always prepare a large batch of this great pareve side dish to keep on hand. It's a great snack from the fridge, a healthy school lunch at room temperature, and a fabulous and trusted Yom Tov side dish.

1. **Prepare the quinoa:** Place quinoa and broth into a medium pot. Bring to a boil over medium-high heat. Cover; simmer for 15 minutes. Remove from heat. Rest 5 minutes. Uncover, fluff with a fork. Transfer to a large bowl.

2. **Prepare the vegetables:** Preheat oven to broil. Line a baking sheet with parchment paper. Coat with cooking spray.

3. Slice ¼-inch from the top and bottom of each pepper. Remove and discard core and seeds; cut each pepper into 4 pieces. Lay flat on prepared baking sheet.

4. Using a sharp paring knife, cut a 1-inch dice pattern into the flesh of the eggplant and zucchinis, being careful to cut down ¼-inch but not through the skin. Place eggplant and zucchinis flesh-side up onto the baking sheet. Place onion slices on baking sheet.

5. Smear olive oil over all the vegetables, brushing additional oil over the eggplant, which is more absorbent. Sprinkle with salt and pepper. Place baking sheet on middle shelf of oven; broil for 10 minutes. After 10 minutes, turn over all vegetables; broil for 5 more minutes. Remove from oven; let cool.

6. Once vegetables are cool enough to handle, scoop eggplant flesh out of skin and cut into 1-inch chunks, using cut marks as a guide. Slice zucchinis and peppers into 1-inch pieces; quarter each onion round. Add vegetables into prepared quinoa.

7. **Prepare the dressing:** Whisk together all dressing ingredients. Pour over quinoa and roasted vegetables. Toss before serving.

— Note —

This refrigerates beautifully and can also be served room temperature.

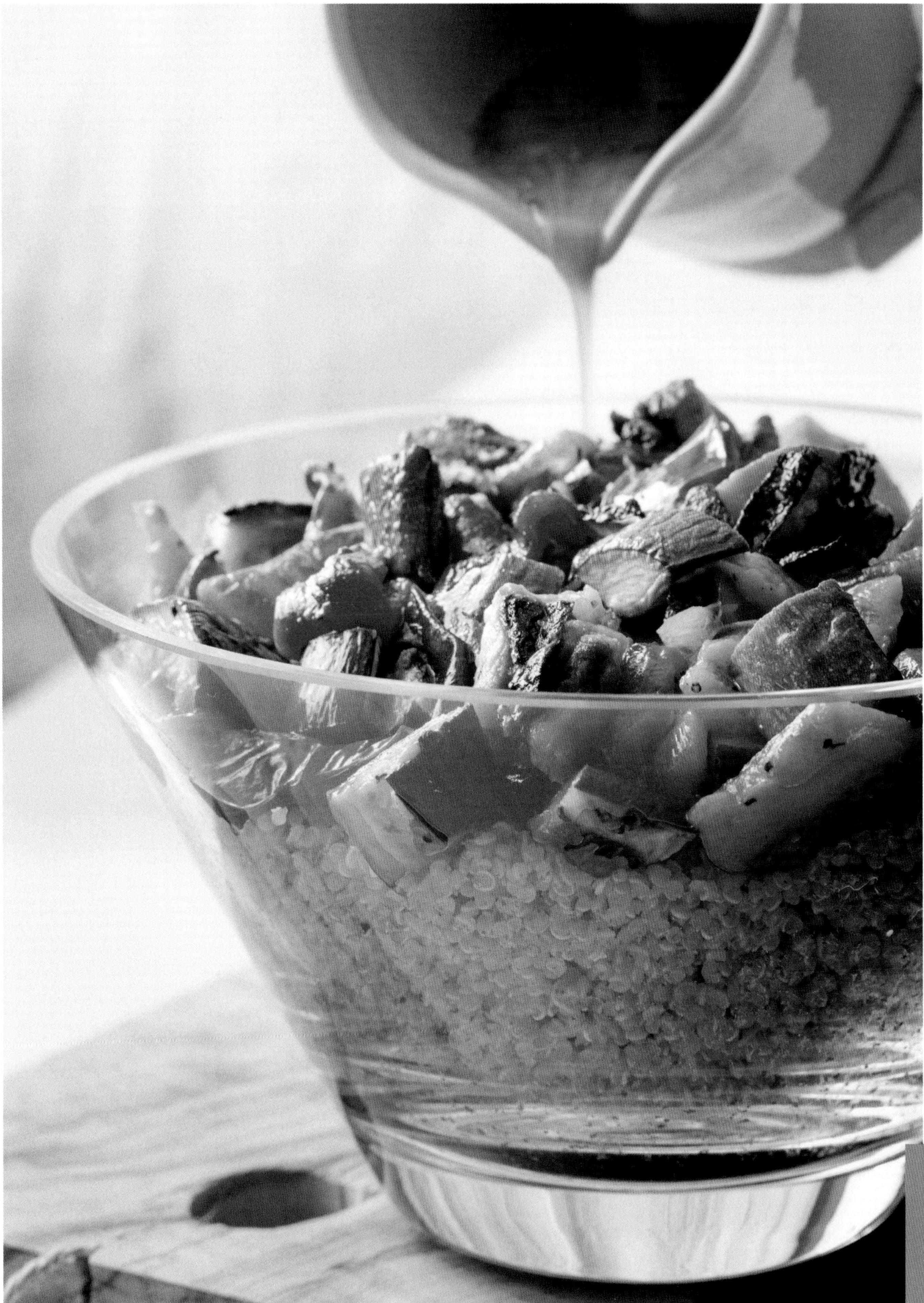

NUTTY LO MEIN

Pareve   YIELDS *8 servings*

You'll "go nuts" for this dish! The perfect blend of sweet and heat is really something unique.

8 oz	spaghetti, regular *or* whole wheat
2 Tbsp	canola oil
1 bunch	scallions, white and light green parts only, sliced
3 cloves	garlic, crushed
3 Tbsp	low sodium soy sauce
2 Tbsp	honey
1 cup	water
1 Tbsp	pareve consommé powder
1 Tbsp	cornstarch
½ cup	chipotle peanuts *or* any spicy nuts
½ cup	honey roasted cashews *or* honey glazed pecans

1. Prepare spaghetti according to package directions; drain and set aside.

2. In a large skillet, heat oil over medium-low heat; add scallions and garlic. Sauté for 3 minutes. Stir in soy sauce and honey.

3. Mix water with consommé powder; add cornstarch. Stir into scallion mixture; continue stirring until mixture thickens.

4. Stir in prepared pasta. Add nuts; toss to combine.

GARLICKY BEEF RICE

Meat **YIELDS** *6-8 servings*

2 cups	water
1 cup	basmati rice
2 Tbsp	beef broth powder
2 Tbsp	canola oil
1 small	onion, diced finely
1 tsp	kosher salt
¼ tsp	black pepper
½ lb	ground beef
8 cloves	garlic, crushed
1 Tbsp	dried parsley flakes *or* **3 Tbsp** fresh parsley, chopped *or* **3 cubes** frozen parsley

A welcome change from the same old, same old. With the addition of garlicky ground beef, plain rice becomes something really delicious.

1. In a medium saucepan, bring water to a boil. Add basmati rice and beef broth powder. Stir to combine; return to a boil. Reduce heat, cover, and simmer for 20 minutes. Remove from heat.

2. In a large skillet, heat oil over medium-high heat; add onion, salt, and black pepper; brown for 5 minutes, stirring occasionally. Add ground beef and crushed garlic. Brown until beef is cooked through, 5–7 minutes.

3. Add parsley flakes and rice; stir to combine.

—Variation

Any type of rice can be used for this dish. Refer to package directions and adjust cooking time accordingly.

Desserts

CRANSICLE

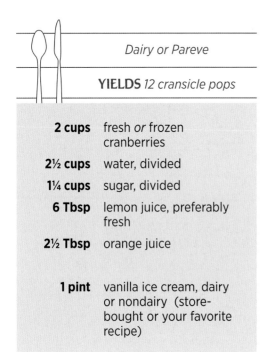

Dairy or Pareve

YIELDS *12 cransicle pops*

2 cups	fresh *or* frozen cranberries
2½ cups	water, divided
1¼ cups	sugar, divided
6 Tbsp	lemon juice, preferably fresh
2½ Tbsp	orange juice
1 pint	vanilla ice cream, dairy or nondairy (store-bought or your favorite recipe)

Ever since I was a little girl, my favorite summer treat has always been the refreshing creamsicle. This inspired me to recreate my childhood favorite ... with a twist.

1. In a medium saucepan over medium-high heat, bring cranberries and 1 cup water to a boil. Stir in ¼ cup sugar. Lower heat; simmer for 10 minutes. Use an immersion blender right in the pot, puree the mixture; chill.

2. In a small saucepan over medium heat, combine remaining water and sugar until sugar is dissolved; bring syrup to a boil, stirring occasionally. Simmer 3 minutes; allow to cool to room temperature.

3. Stir together cooled cranberry puree, cooled syrup, lemon juice, and orange juice. Use immersion blender to puree again. Transfer to a 2-quart freezer-proof container; freeze for 3 hours.

4. Remove from freezer; puree again. Return to freezer overnight.

5. **To assemble:** Allow cranberry sorbet to soften slightly. Set out a 12-cup pop mold. Spoon each pop mold ⅔ full with sorbet. Freeze for 2 hours.

6. Allow ice cream to soften. Remove mold from freezer. Spoon ice cream into molds, filling to the top of each mold. Place cover on each mold; press sorbet pop stick into the center. Freeze until firm.

7. **To serve:** Place mold in water for a minute for ease in releasing each pop.

— Variation

You can also serve this dessert in dessert dishes, plating a scoop of sorbet and a scoop of vanilla ice cream, garnished with fresh fruit.

MOCHA PRALINE ICE CREAM

Pareve **YIELDS** *16 servings*

In my family, this dessert is synonymous with Yom Tov. Even after a big meal, there is always room for this delicacy.

Praline Powder

1 cup	sugar
1 cup	ground almonds

Mocha Ice Cream

6	eggs, separated
1 cup	sugar, divided
2 Tbsp	vanilla sugar, divided
1 (8-oz) container	nondairy whipping cream
1 Tbsp	coffee granules, dissolved in **1 tsp** hot water

Fudge Layer

½ cup (1 stick)	margarine
1½ cups	powdered sugar
3	egg yolks, slightly beaten
2 oz	bittersweet chocolate
2 Tbsp	vanilla extract

— Notes

To serve deconstructed as pictured, freeze ice cream and fudge in separate containers. Fudge will take a few hours to defrost so be sure to take it out of the freezer with enough time to fully defrost before serving. Put a scoop of ice cream into a dessert bowl. Top with 1-2 tablespoons fudge and sprinkle with 1 tablespoon praline powder.

Praline powder can be stored for 2 months at room temperature in an airtight container.

1. **Prepare the praline powder:** Place a sheet of foil on your work surface. Place sugar into a small pan over medium heat. Sugar will slowly dissolve, then change to an amber color. It may take up to 5 minutes for the sugar to dissolve, but watch it carefully because it turns from liquid to amber very quickly and you don't want it to burn. The sugar will melt more smoothly if you don't stir it too much.

2. Once the sugar is mostly liquid and has turned a caramel color, stir in the ground almonds. Pour the mixture onto prepared foil; spread as thin as possible; allow to cool and harden, about 10 minutes. Break brittle into small pieces. Place into a resealable bag and hit with a meat mallet or rolling pin to prepare pieces for the food processor. This will ease the blending process, as large chunks may be too difficult to process. Add pieces to a food processor fitted with the "S" blade. Pulse until a grainy powder forms. Set aside. If making in advance, store in an airtight container or a resealable bag.

3. **Prepare the mocha ice cream:** Set out a 9x13-inch pan.

4. Using an electric mixer on high speed, beat egg yolks in a large bowl until thickened. Gradually add ½ cup sugar and 1 tablespoon vanilla sugar. Beat until light yellow in color. Slowly add nondairy whipping cream; beat until light and fluffy. Fold in coffee; set aside.

5. In a second large bowl, use an electric mixer on high speed to beat the egg whites until soft peaks begin to form. Slowly add remaining ½ cup sugar and remaining 1 tablespoon vanilla sugar. Fold yolk mixture into white mixture until fully incorporated. Pour mixture into prepared pan. Freeze at least 3 hours.

6. **Prepare fudge layer:** In a saucepan over low heat, melt margarine. Add powdered sugar; stir until completely incorporated. Whisk in beaten yolks. Add chocolate and vanilla extract, whisking to combine. Stir until mixture begins to bubble. Remove from heat; cool completely. Pour cold mixture over frozen mocha ice cream. Freeze for 3 hours.

7. Remove from freezer; top with praline powder. Freeze until ready to serve.

POACHED APPLE AND STRAWBERRY SUNDAE

Pareve **YIELDS** *6-8 servings*

This poached apple is anything but ho-hum. It's a refreshingly light finale to any meal that will leave you wishing there was just one more bite.

Strawberry Sauce

1 lb	frozen strawberries
½ cup	sugar
1 tsp	lemon juice, preferably fresh
1 Tbsp	peach schnapps

Poached Apples

4 cups	water
1½ cups	sugar
•	zest of 2 lemons
•	juice of 1 lemon
1	vanilla bean, split lengthwise
4	firm red apples, peeled (Honeycrisp, Pink Lady, Fuji, Gala, *or* Cortland)
•	nondairy vanilla ice cream (store-bought or your favorite recipe), for serving

1. **Prepare the strawberry sauce:** Using a food processor fitted with the "S" blade, puree strawberry sauce ingredients. Transfer to a bowl; cover. Chill mixture for 2 hours.

2. **Prepare the poached apples:** In a medium saucepan, combine water, sugar, lemon zest, lemon juice, and vanilla bean. Bring mixture to a boil over medium-high heat. Stir until the sugar has dissolved and syrup forms. Simmer syrup for 5 minutes.

3. Place apples into the syrup; poach apples over a low simmer, covered, for 8 minutes. Remove from heat. Allow apples to cool in the syrup. Remove and discard vanilla bean. Slice apples into thin wedges.

4. **To serve:** Fan apple wedges around the bottom of dessert glasses. Place a scoop of ice cream on apple wedges. Pour strawberry puree over the ice cream. You may have extra puree, which may be frozen for future use.

MINI APPLE AND BLUEBERRY CRISPS

Pareve

YIELDS *10 large ramekins*

A nice new twist to an old-fashioned classic.

½ **cup**	seedless raspberry jam
•	zest of 1 lemon
2 Tbsp	freshly squeezed lemon juice
¼ **cup**	sugar
¼ **cup**	light brown sugar
1½-2 Tbsp	cornstarch
⅛ **tsp**	sea salt
4	apples, peeled and diced (2 Granny Smith, 2 Golden Delicious)
2 cups	fresh *or* frozen blueberries
•	nondairy vanilla ice cream (store-bought or your favorite recipe), for serving, optional

Streusel Crumbs

¾ **cup**	flour
⅓ **cup**	light brown sugar, packed
2 Tbsp	sugar
1 Tbsp	vanilla sugar
4 Tbsp	canola oil

1. Preheat oven to 350°F. Coat 10 large ramekins with cooking spray. Prepare a baking sheet.

2. **Prepare streusel crumbs:** Mix all streusel ingredients together by hand until crumbs form; set aside.

3. **Prepare the mini apple blueberry pies:** In a small bowl, whisk raspberry jam until smooth. Add lemon zest and lemon juice. In a second bowl, combine sugars, cornstarch, and salt. Toss in apples and blueberries. Add raspberry jam mixture. Toss to combine. Place ½ cup apple mixture into each ramekin. Top with 2 heaping tablespoons streusel crumbs.

4. Place ramekins on prepared baking sheet. Bake 35-40 minutes on center rack.

5. Serve warm or at room temperature with a scoop of ice cream, if desired.

VANILLA RUM CREPES WITH NUT DRIZZLE

Pareve **YIELDS** *12 servings*

On a scale of 1-10, the presentation and taste of this dessert are an 11!

Crepes

1½ cups	almond *or* coconut milk
2 Tbsp	vanilla extract
2 Tbsp	rum
3	egg yolks
2 Tbsp	sugar
1 tsp	sea salt
1½ cups	sifted flour
5 Tbsp	margarine, melted
¼ cup	canola oil, for frying

Apricot Filling

1 cup	apricot jam
½ cup	ground almonds
½ cup	sugar

Nut Topping

½ cup	pure maple syrup
½ cup	light corn syrup
¼-½ tsp	vanilla extract
½ tsp	kosher salt
1 cup	pecan halves

- nondairy vanilla ice cream (store-bought *or* your favorite recipe), for serving
- powdered sugar, for serving

1. **Prepare nut topping:** In a small saucepan over medium heat, bring maple syrup and corn syrup to a boil. Add vanilla and salt. Remove from heat. Add pecans to the pan; stir to coat completely. Allow mixture to cool for 30 minutes.

2. **Prepare the crepes:** In a medium bowl, use an immersion blender to blend together almond milk, vanilla, rum, egg yolks, sugar, salt, flour, and melted margarine. Refrigerate batter for 30 minutes.

3. Cover a kitchen towel with paper towels. Heat a 6-inch skillet over medium-high heat. Dip a paper towel into oil; grease skillet with the oily paper towel; heat through.

4. Working quickly, pour ¼ cup crepe batter into the center of the pan. Tilt pan in all directions to spread batter evenly. Cook until edges of crepe begin to lift, about 1 minute. Shake pan sharply back and forth to loosen the crepe. Lift an edge; turn crepe. Cook for 30 seconds.

5. Slide the finished crepe onto prepared towel. Repeat with remaining batter, re-greasing pan as necessary.

6. **Prepare the apricot filling:** In a small pot over medium heat or in the microwave in a microwave-safe bowl, melt the apricot jam. In a small bowl, combine almonds and sugar.

7. Brush each crepe with apricot jam, leaving a 1-inch border. Sprinkle 1-2 tablespoons of almond/sugar mixture over jam. Fold the crepe in half; then fold in half again.

8. **To serve:** Place 2 crepes on each plate. Plate a scoop of ice cream on the side. Drizzle with 1 tablespoon nut topping. Sprinkle with powdered sugar.

— Note

Crepes freeze beautifully.

CUSTARD FRUIT TARTS

Pareve **YIELDS** *10 mini tarts*

As a newlywed, I often made these minis as one 9-inch tart. Because I love variety, I retired it in favor of other desserts. While going through my archives, I stumbled upon this recipe and remembered how much we always loved it. I wonder how I could have ever forgotten it!

Tart Shell

1½ cups	flour
1½ Tbsp	sugar
½ tsp	sea salt
½ cup (1 stick)	margarine, cold, cut into chunks
2 Tbsp	cold water
1	egg yolk

Custard Filling

2 Tbsp	flour
½ cup	sugar
1 Tbsp	cornstarch
2 cups	almond milk *or* nondairy whipping cream
3	egg yolks
1 tsp	vanilla extract
½ cup	nondairy whipping cream

Topping

1 pint	strawberries, hulled and halved
1 pint	blueberries
2-3	kiwis, peeled and sliced
½ cup	pomegranate seeds
¼ cup	apricot preserves

—Variation—

Instead of making mini tarts, you can make one big tart in a 11-inch round tart shell. Double the baking time for the large tart shell.

1. **Prepare the tart shell:** In a medium bowl, use your hands or a pastry cutter to combine flour, sugar, salt, and margarine until fine crumbs form. Add egg yolk and water; work the mixture until a dough forms. Shape into a ball; cover with plastic wrap. Refrigerate for 1 hour.

2. Preheat oven to 325°F. Set out a baking sheet and 10 (3-inch) rectangular tart pans with removable bottoms.

3. Place dough on a well-floured surface; flour a rolling pin. Divide dough into 10 portions. Roll each portion into a rectangle.

4. Press dough into and up the sides of prepared tart pans. Cover dough with foil, pressing down on the foil so it molds to the shape of the pan; fill with pie weights or uncooked rice or beans. (This will prevent the dough from shrinking during baking.) Place filled tart pans on prepared baking sheet; bake for 12 minutes.

5. Remove the baked shells from the oven; remove the weights and the foil. Return the shells to the oven for 7-8 minutes until they are a light golden brown. Remove from oven; set aside to cool completely.

6. **Prepare the custard filling:** In a 2-quart saucepan, combine flour, sugar, and cornstarch. Using a whisk, beat in almond milk and egg yolks. Cook over medium heat, stirring constantly, until mixture boils and thickens, about 3 minutes. Cook for 1 minute more. Remove from heat; stir in vanilla.

7. Transfer custard to a large bowl. Cover surface of custard with plastic wrap; refrigerate for 3 hours.

8. Using an electric mixer on medium speed, beat whipping cream until stiff peaks form. Fold whipped cream into chilled custard. Fill tart shells with custard filling. Refrigerate until firm, about 1 hour.

9. **To serve:** Arrange strawberries and blueberries over the custard filling. In the microwave in a microwave-safe bowl, heat apricot preserves until smooth and spreadable. Brush over the fruit to give it a shiny glaze.

MACADAMIA CARAMEL TART

Pareve **YIELDS** *8-10 servings*

All of my favorite flavors rolled into one dessert. Yum!

Shortbread Crust

1½ cups	sifted flour
¼ tsp	sea salt
¼ tsp	baking powder
6 Tbsp **(¾ stick)**	margarine, softened, at room temperature
3 Tbsp	sugar
1	egg
¼ tsp	vanilla extract

Macadamia Caramel Filling

8 Tbsp	margarine, softened, at room temperature
2 Tbsp	honey
½ cup	light brown sugar
2 Tbsp	sugar
pinch	sea salt
2 Tbsp	nondairy whipping cream
1 cup	macadamia nuts, coarsely chopped

Chocolate Ganache

¼ cup	nondairy whipping cream
2 oz	bittersweet chocolate, finely chopped
1 tsp	light corn syrup

Whipped Cream

8 oz	nondairy whipping cream
½ cup	powdered sugar
1 tsp	vanilla extract
•	cocoa, for garnish

1. Preheat oven to 350°F. Set out a 9-inch fluted tart pan with a removable bottom.

2. **Prepare the shortbread crust:** In a small bowl, combine flour, salt, and baking powder; set aside.

3. Using an electric mixer on medium speed, cream margarine and sugar until light and fluffy. Add egg and vanilla. Mix on low speed until combined. Slowly add flour mixture, mixing until dough starts to come together. Remove dough from bowl; fashion into a ball.

4. Transfer dough to prepared tart pan. With your fingertips, press the dough evenly into the bottom and up the sides of the pan. Set crust aside.

5. **Prepare macadamia caramel filling:** In a small saucepan over medium-high heat, stir together margarine, honey, sugars, and salt. Stir constantly until mixture comes to a boil (about 3 minutes). Remove pan from heat; stir in whipping cream and nuts.

6. Pour filling into prepared crust; bake for 30 minutes.

7. Cool tart on a wire rack for 1 hour.

8. **Prepare chocolate ganache:** In a small saucepan over medium heat, bring whipping cream to a boil. Remove pan from heat; stir in chocolate and corn syrup. Whisk until mixture is smooth.

9. Pour glaze over the cooled tart, working fast as ganache sets and hardens quickly; use an offset spatula to spread evenly. Refrigerate tart, uncovered, until chocolate layer is set.

10. **Prepare the whipped cream:** Using an electric mixer, beat the whipping cream to form soft peaks. Add powdered sugar and vanilla. Continue to beat until stiff peaks form.

11. Remove tart from refrigerator. Serve each piece with a dollop of whipped cream and garnish with cocoa.

SILKY CHOCOLATE MOUSSE TART

Pareve **YIELDS** *8-10 servings*

A chocolate lover's delight!

8 oz quality pareve chocolate, such as Noblesse

2½ cups nondairy whipping cream, divided

1 chocolate pie crust (page 264)

2 Tbsp powdered sugar

½ tsp vanilla extract

½ Tbsp rum

2 oz chocolate, for garnish, optional

1. Chop chocolate finely; place into a large bowl. Set aside.

2. In a small saucepan, over medium-high heat, bring 1 cup whipping cream to a boil. Pour heated cream over chopped chocolate; stir until chocolate is melted and smooth. Transfer chocolate mixture to a large bowl, reserving ⅓ cup mixture in the small saucepan.

3. Add ½ cup remaining whipping cream to the bowl. Stir until blended. Refrigerate for 1 hour.

4. Once chocolate mixture has cooled, transfer to a large bowl. Using an electric mixer, on high speed, whip for 30 seconds. In a second bowl, whip up ½ cup remaining whipping cream to form stiff peaks. Fold whipped cream into chocolate mixture. Spread into the prepared pie crust; use an offset spatula to smooth the top.

5. Place saucepan of reserved chocolate mixture over low heat. Heat through. Pour chocolate glaze over mousse; use an offset spatula to spread quickly.

6. Pour remaining ½ cup whipping cream into clean mixer bowl. Add powdered sugar, vanilla, and rum. Using an electric mixer, whip to form high peaks. Transfer to a piping bag fitted with a star tip. Pipe rosettes around the perimeter of the tart, or simply drop tablespoons of whip around the perimeter.

7. **Prepare optional chocolate garnish:** Line a baking sheet with parchment paper.

8. Place 2 ounces chocolate into a resealable bag. Using the microwave, at 20 second intervals, melt chocolate in a microwave-safe bowl. Mix well after each interval. Snip the corner of the bag; pipe 12 (2-inch) rosettes onto prepared baking sheet. Refrigerate until chocolate sets.

9. Evenly place chocolate rosettes around the tart.

10. Refrigerate until serving.

CHOCOLATE BOURBON PECAN PIE

Pareve **YIELDS** *8-10 servings*

I have not always been a pecan pie fan. I decided to play with the flavors and bump it up a notch. With the addition of the bourbon and melted chocolate, I am sold — and I hope you will be, too.

Chocolate Pie Crust

1 cup	flour
⅓ cup	cocoa powder
⅓ cup	powdered sugar
6 Tbsp (¾ stick)	margarine
2 Tbsp	water

Pecan Filling

3 Tbsp	margarine, melted
3½ oz	quality pareve chocolate, such as Noblesse, cut into chunks
1 cup	sugar
3 Tbsp	light brown sugar
½ tsp	sea salt
1 cup	dark corn syrup
¾ tsp	vanilla extract
3	eggs, beaten
2 Tbsp	bourbon
1 heaping cup	pecan halves

1. Prepare a 9-inch round pan.

2. **Prepare the chocolate pie crust:** In a large bowl, combine flour, cocoa powder, and powdered sugar. Using a pastry cutter or 2 knives, cut in margarine until crumbs form. Add water; knead by hand until a dough forms.

3. Form the dough into a ball; place between 2 sheets of parchment paper. Roll out into a 12-inch circle. Press dough into prepared pan. To avoid shrinkage, use a fork to poke holes into the sides and bottom of the crust.

4. Preheat oven to 350°F.

5. **Prepare the pecan filling:** In a double boiler or in the microwave in a microwave-safe bowl at 20-second intervals, melt together margarine and chocolate. In a large bowl, combine chocolate mixture with sugars, salt, corn syrup, vanilla, eggs, and bourbon.

6. Arrange pecans in the unbaked pie crust. Carefully, so as not to move the nuts, pour chocolate mixture over pecans. Cover pan loosely with foil; bake for 35 minutes.

7. Remove foil; return to oven and bake an additional 20 minutes.

8. The center will be a little jiggly and will continue to set as it cools. If the whole pie is still very jiggly, cover the pan loosely with foil; bake up to an additional 20 minutes. (The baking time for this pie can vary from 55-75 minutes.)

9. Allow to cool at room temperature, then refrigerate until serving. The pie is best served chilled.

---Note---

Do not use light corn syrup in these recipe. It has a thinner consistency and won't yield optimal results.

WHITE CHOCOLATE CHEESECAKE

Dairy **YIELDS** *14-16 servings*

I have never met a cheesecake that I didn't like. This New York-style white chocolate cheesecake can only be described with one word: perfection.

Shortbread Cookie Crust

6 oz	shortbread cookies
2 Tbsp	butter, melted

Chocolate Ganache

2 oz	dark chocolate
4 Tbsp	heavy cream
1 tsp	light corn syrup

Cheesecake Filling

3 (3½-oz) bars	dairy white chocolate, finely chopped
½ cup	heavy cream
3 (8-oz) bars	cream cheese, at room temperature
½ cup	sugar
4	eggs, at room temperature
1 Tbsp	vanilla extract
½ cup	sour cream

Cream Cheese Frosting

8 oz (2 sticks)	butter, softened
1 (8-oz) bar	cream cheese, chilled
2¼ cups	powdered sugar
2 Tbsp	heavy cream
2 tsp	vanilla extract

1. **Prepare the shortbread cookie crust:** Coat bottom and sides of a 9-inch springform pan with cooking spray. Place shortbread cookies into a resealable bag. Use your hands or a rolling pin to crush to fine crumbs. Add melted butter; mix well. Press cookie crumbs onto the bottom of the prepared pan. Bake for 10 minutes. Remove from oven.

2. **Prepare the chocolate ganache:** In the microwave, melt chocolate in a microwave-safe bowl at 15-second intervals, stirring well between intervals, until completely melted and smooth. Add heavy cream and corn syrup. Mix until smooth and glossy.

3. Pour ganache over shortbread crust; spread evenly. (To spread ganache evenly, you may lift the pan and rotate it side to side until completely coated.) Place pan in freezer while you prepare cheesecake filling.

4. Preheat oven to 325°F. Wrap 3 large pieces of foil around the bottom and up the outside of the springform pan so that it is waterproof.

5. **Prepare the cheesecake filling:** In a double boiler or in the microwave in a microwave-safe bowl at 15-second intervals, melt white chocolate, stirring well between intervals, until completely melted and smooth. Add heavy cream. Stir until smooth.

6. Using an electric mixer, beat cream cheese until smooth. Add sugar. Mix until blended. Add eggs, one at a time, beating for 30 seconds between each addition. Add white chocolate mixture and vanilla. Beat until blended and smooth. Add sour cream. Continue to beat just until smooth. Do not overbeat.

7. Remove pan from freezer. Pour filling over ganache layer. Tap pan on counter to level mixture and release any air bubbles.

8. Place wrapped pan into a larger pan (double steamer size); place pan on center rack of oven. Fill larger pan halfway with water. Bake for 1 hour. Top will be golden.

9. Turn off heat. Open oven door; leave cheesecake in the oven for 30 minutes.

10. Remove cake from oven. Remove foil wrapping and wipe moisture from outside of pan. Refrigerate overnight.

11. Carefully run a knife around the edges of the cake before releasing the sides of the pan.

12. **Prepare the cream cheese frosting:** Using an electric mixer on medium speed, beat together butter and cream cheese until smooth. Scrape down the sides. Gradually add powdered sugar; beat until combined. Scrape down sides again; add heavy cream and vanilla extract. Beat until combined.

13. **Garnish cheesecake:** Spread a very thin layer of frosting over the top of the cake. Add frosting to a pastry bag fitted with a star tip; pipe rosettes around rim of cake or to cover the entire top. Alternatively, spread frosting over cake with an icing spreader or offset spatula.

CRÈME BRÛLÉE

A delicate sweet cream and crispy caramelized sugar topping is the key to a true crème brulee. It was a real challenge to make my husband's all-time favorite dessert delicious and yet pareve. I believe this one was worth the effort. BB, this one's for you.

Pareve **YIELDS** *6 servings*

2 cups almond creamer *or* coconut creamer (see Note)

1 vanilla bean *or* **1 Tbsp** vanilla extract *or* **1 Tbsp** vanilla bean paste

5 egg yolks

1 egg

½ cup sugar

Topping

4 tsp sugar

2 tsp vanilla sugar

1. Preheat oven to 325°F. Set out 6 (4-oz.) ramekins and a 9x13-inch baking pan.

2. Pour nondairy creamer into a medium saucepan. Split the vanilla bean lengthwise down the center; scrape seeds out with the tip of a knife. Add vanilla seeds to creamer. Heat over medium heat until small bubbles appear at the edge of the pot (do not bring to a boil); remove from heat.

3. In a medium bowl, whisk together egg yolks, egg, and sugar. Slowly add heated cream, whisking constantly (it is important to add hot cream slowly to avoid scrambling the eggs).

4. Divide mixture evenly between prepared ramekins. Optional but highly recommended: To obtain optimal smooth results, pour mixture through a small fine strainer when pouring into ramekins.

5. Gently place ramekins into prepared baking pan. Place onto oven rack. Pour 1-inch boiling water into the pan. Bake 30-35 minutes, until custard is set. Custard will still be a little jiggly; it will continue to set as it cools. Refrigerate for 2 hours. If preparing in advance see Note.

6. Preheat oven to hi-broil.

7. **Prepare the topping:** In a small bowl, combine sugars. Evenly cover the entire top of each ramekin with 1 teaspoon sugar mixture. Broil 2-3 minutes. Remove from oven.

—Note

This recipe can be prepared to Step 6 up to 3 days in advance. If preparing in advance, cover with plastic wrap until ready to serve. At this point make sure the surface is moisture free, blotting with a paper towel if necessary, add the sugar, and continue with Step 6.

You can substitute nondairy whipped topping for the nondairy almond or coconut creamer.

STICKY TOFFEE PUDDING CAKES

Pareve   **YIELDS** *8 ramekins*

This classic English dessert was shared with me by my sister-in-law Judy, who hails from the UK. No one will ever believe that the secret to this outstanding dessert comes from the natural sweetness of delicious dates!

1 cup	pitted dates, finely chopped
¾ cup	boiling water
1 tsp	vanilla extract
6 Tbsp (**¾ stick**)	margarine
⅔ cup	turbinado sugar (see Note on page 44)
2	eggs
2 Tbsp	dark corn syrup
1 cup	self-rising flour *or* **1 cup** flour + **1 tsp** baking powder
1 tsp	baking soda
½ cup	almond *or* coconut milk
•	nondairy vanilla ice cream, optional

Toffee Sauce

1 cup	dark brown sugar, packed
4 Tbsp	margarine
½ cup	nondairy whipping cream *or* cream of coconut, divided
1 Tbsp	dark corn syrup

1. Preheat oven to 350°F. Adjust oven rack to middle position. Grease and flour 8 (4-oz) ramekins.

2. Pour hot water over the chopped dates; let soak for 5 minutes. Transfer mixture to a food processor fitted with the "S" blade; pulse until smooth. Add vanilla extract. Set aside.

3. Using an electric mixer on medium speed, beat margarine and sugar until slightly creamy. Add eggs, 1 at a time, beating well between each addition. Beat in corn syrup.

4. In a small bowl, combine flour and baking soda. Alternate adding flour mixture and almond milk into the margarine/sugar mixture until batter is smooth. Do not overbeat.

5. Stir date mixture into the batter. Mixture may look curdled at this point. Evenly divide batter between ramekins.

6. Bake 20-25 minutes until cakes have risen and are firm. Remove ramekins from oven; cool 10 minutes.

7. **Prepare the toffee sauce:** In a medium saucepan, combine sugar, margarine, and ¼ cup whipping cream. Bring mixture to a boil over medium heat, stirring constantly until the sugar has dissolved. Stir in corn syrup. Raise heat; bring mixture to a boil, stirring occasionally, for 2-3 minutes, until it turns a toffee color. Take care not to burn it. Remove pan from heat. Mix in remaining ¼ cup whipping cream.

8. Using a toothpick, poke holes in the cakes. Pour 1-2 tablespoons toffee sauce over each ramekin; allow to settle for 5 minutes.

9. **To serve:** Heat remaining toffee sauce. Pour 1-2 tablespoons sauce over each ramekin. Serve with a scoop of vanilla ice cream. You may drizzle with chocolate syrup or remaining toffee sauce. If you prefer, invert the cakes out of the ramekins onto individual plates before serving.

Note

The cakes can be made through Step 8 and stored covered on the counter overnight, refrigerated for a week, or frozen for a month. Toffee sauce can be stored in the fridge for up to a month.

Baked Goods

LOTUS RIBBON BUNDT CAKE

Parave **YIELDS** *12 servings*

My top criteria for a perfect cake are moist texture and fabulous flavor. Achieving this combination was not easy. After many trials, I took one bite and knew this one was a keeper. This "honey" cake is a great idea to make for Rosh Hashanah.

Lotus Filling

¾ cup	crushed Lotus cookie crumbs (14 cookies)
1 oz	bittersweet chocolate, grated

Cake

2 cups	flour
½ cup (1 [3.5-oz] package)	vanilla instant pudding mix
1 tsp	sea salt
1 tsp	baking powder
½ tsp	baking soda
¾ cup	orange juice
¼ cup	honey
¼ cup	bourbon
1 Tbsp	vanilla extract
¾ cup	canola oil
1¾ cups	sugar
4	eggs

Chocolate Glaze

3.5 oz	bittersweet chocolate, very finely diced or grated
¼ cup	almond creamer *or* nondairy whipping cream, hot
2 Tbsp	light corn syrup
¼ tsp	vanilla extract
pinch	sea salt

1. Adjust oven rack to middle-lower rack. Preheat oven to 350°F. Grease and flour a 12-cup Bundt pan; set aside.

2. **Prepare the Lotus filling:** In a small bowl, toss together cookie crumbs and grated chocolate. Set aside.

3. **Prepare the cake:** In a medium bowl, whisk together flour, pudding mix, salt, baking powder, and baking soda. In a small bowl, whisk together orange juice, honey, bourbon, and vanilla extract. Set bowls aside.

4. In the large bowl of an electric mixer at medium speed, beat together oil and sugar until combined. Add eggs, one at a time, beating until light and fluffy.

5. Lower mixer speed; beat in ⅓ flour mixture, followed by ½ liquid mixture. Beat in remaining flour and liquid mixtures until just combined.

6. Pour half the batter into the prepared pan. Smooth the top. Sprinkle evenly with filling. Pour remaining batter over filling. Gently tap the pan on the counter to settle the batter. Bake for 50-60 minutes, until a toothpick inserted into cake comes out clean with a few moist crumbs.

7. Allow cake to cool 10 minutes, then turn out onto a cooling rack. Allow cake to cool 2 hours. Transfer to cake plate.

8. **Prepare the chocolate glaze:** In a medium bowl, whisk all glaze ingredients together until smooth. Allow to set and thicken for 25 minutes. Pour over completely cooled cake. Allow glaze to set before serving.

— Note —

This recipe is freezer friendly!

DOUBLE CHOCOLATE PUDDING BROWNIES

Pareve **YIELDS** *16 brownies*

Fudgy, dense, and gooey, these brownies are a moist, double-chocolatey treat. What a chocolicious delight!

3.5 oz	better quality chocolate, such as Noblesse
1 stick (½ cup)	margarine
3 large	eggs
1 cup	sugar
2 tsp	vanilla extract
½ tsp	sea salt
½ cup (1 [3.5-oz] package)	chocolate instant pudding mix
1 cup	flour
½-⅔ cup	chocolate chips, optional

1. Preheat oven to 350°F. Grease and flour an 8-inch square pan.

2. Melt chocolate and margarine over a double boiler, or in a microwave-safe bowl in the microwave at 20 second intervals, stirring in between. Set aside.

3. In a medium bowl, whisk eggs, sugar, vanilla, and salt until slightly thickened. Slowly add warm melted chocolate mixture, flour, and pudding mix. Continue to whisk or stir with a wooden spoon until well mixed.

4. Transfer batter to prepared pan. Sprinkle chocolate chips on top, if desired.

5. Bake 25-30 minutes, until mostly set. Brownies will continue to set as they cool.

— Note —————————————

If using a disposable pan, you may need an additional 5 minutes bake time.

This recipe is freezer friendly!

BLUEBERRY LEMON LOAF

Pareve **YIELDS** *12 servings*

This easy loaf cake is a delicious combination of lemon and blueberry flavors. It is a wonderful addition to the ever-popular blueberry muffin family.

Batter

1½ cups	flour
¾ cup	sugar
½ tsp	sea salt
2 tsp	baking powder
¼ cup	canola oil
¼ cup	fresh lemon juice
¼ cup	coconut milk *or* other nondairy milk
1	egg
1¼ cups	blueberries, fresh or frozen

Lemon Crumble

⅓ cup	sugar
½ cup	flour
1 Tbsp	vanilla sugar
3 Tbsp	canola oil
•	zest of 1 lemon, preferably fresh

1. Preheat oven to 350°F. Grease and flour well a medium loaf pan.

2. **Prepare the lemon crumble:** In a medium bowl, combine all crumble ingredients to form coarse crumbs.

3. **Prepare the blueberry lemon loaf:** Mix all batter ingredients except blueberries in a large mixing bowl (by hand). Gently fold in blueberries. If using frozen blueberries, do not defrost before using. Transfer batter to loaf pan; sprinkle crumble evenly over batter.

4. Bake 45–50 minutes. Test for doneness by inserting a toothpick and checking that it comes out clean. Cool completely.

─**Tip**─

To prevent the blueberry juices from running, toss blueberries in 2 tablespoons flour. This coating will create a barrier that prevents the juices from running into and streaking the batter.

─**Note**─

This recipe is freezer friendly!

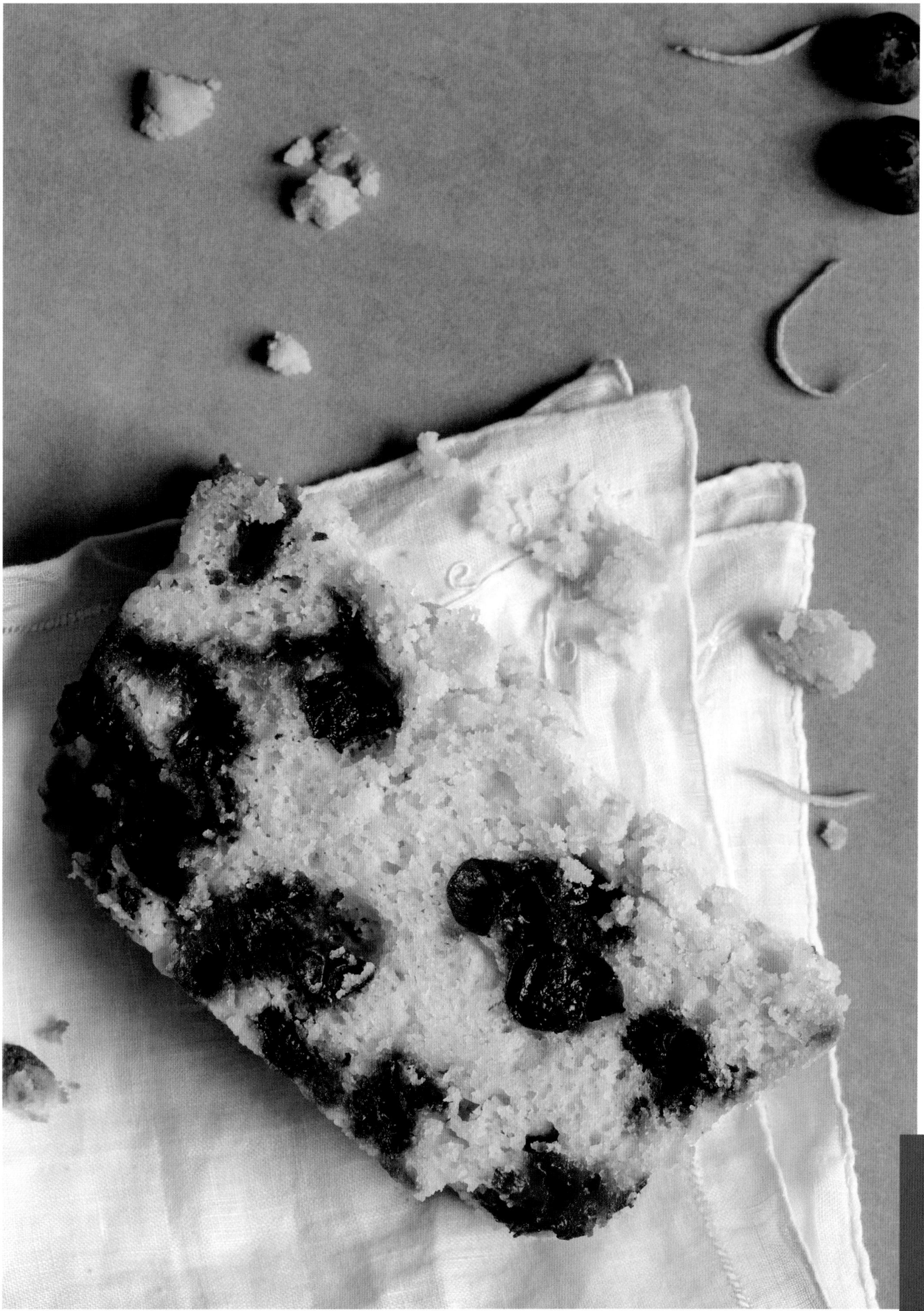

FRENCH COFFEE CAKE MUFFINS

Pareve **YIELDS** *12 muffins*

There's nothing like starting your day with a cup of coffee and this perfect coffee cake muffin. This easy, no-mixer recipe yields the moistest no-fail muffins ever.

Crumb and Topping

⅔ cup	flour
1 cup	dark brown sugar
2 tsp	cinnamon
½ cup	finely chopped pecans, optional
1 Tbsp	vanilla sugar
⅓ cup	canola oil

Muffin Batter

5 Tbsp	canola oil
1 tsp	vanilla extract
¾ cup	sugar
1	egg
½ cup	almond milk *or* any nondairy milk
2 cups	flour
2 tsp	baking powder
½ tsp	sea salt
•	powdered sugar, for sprinkling, optional

1. Preheat oven to 375°F. Grease and flour 1 (12-cup) cupcake pan or a medium loaf pan.

2. **Prepare the crumb and topping:** In a small bowl, mix together flour, sugar, cinnamon, pecans, and vanilla sugar. Add oil; mix by hand or with a fork until coarse crumbs form. Set aside.

3. **Prepare the muffin batter:** In a large bowl, whisk together oil, sugar, and vanilla (the mixture will be crumbly). Add egg; whisk until smooth.

4. In a medium bowl, whisk together flour, baking powder, and salt. Alternate adding dry ingredients and nondairy milk into the mixture in the large bowl, whisking well between each addition.

5. Place a heaping tablespoon batter into each prepared muffin cup. Sprinkle with 1 tablespoon crumbs. Place another heaping tablespoon batter over the crumbs; top with a second tablespoon crumbs. Bake for 30 minutes. Allow to cool. Alternatively, pour half the batter into prepared loaf pan. Sprinkle with half the crumbs. Pour remaining batter over the crumbs; top with remaining crumbs. Bake for 60 minutes. Allow to cool.

6. Sprinkle cooled muffins with powdered sugar.

— **Note** —

For moister muffins, bake at 350°F.

This recipe is freezer friendly!

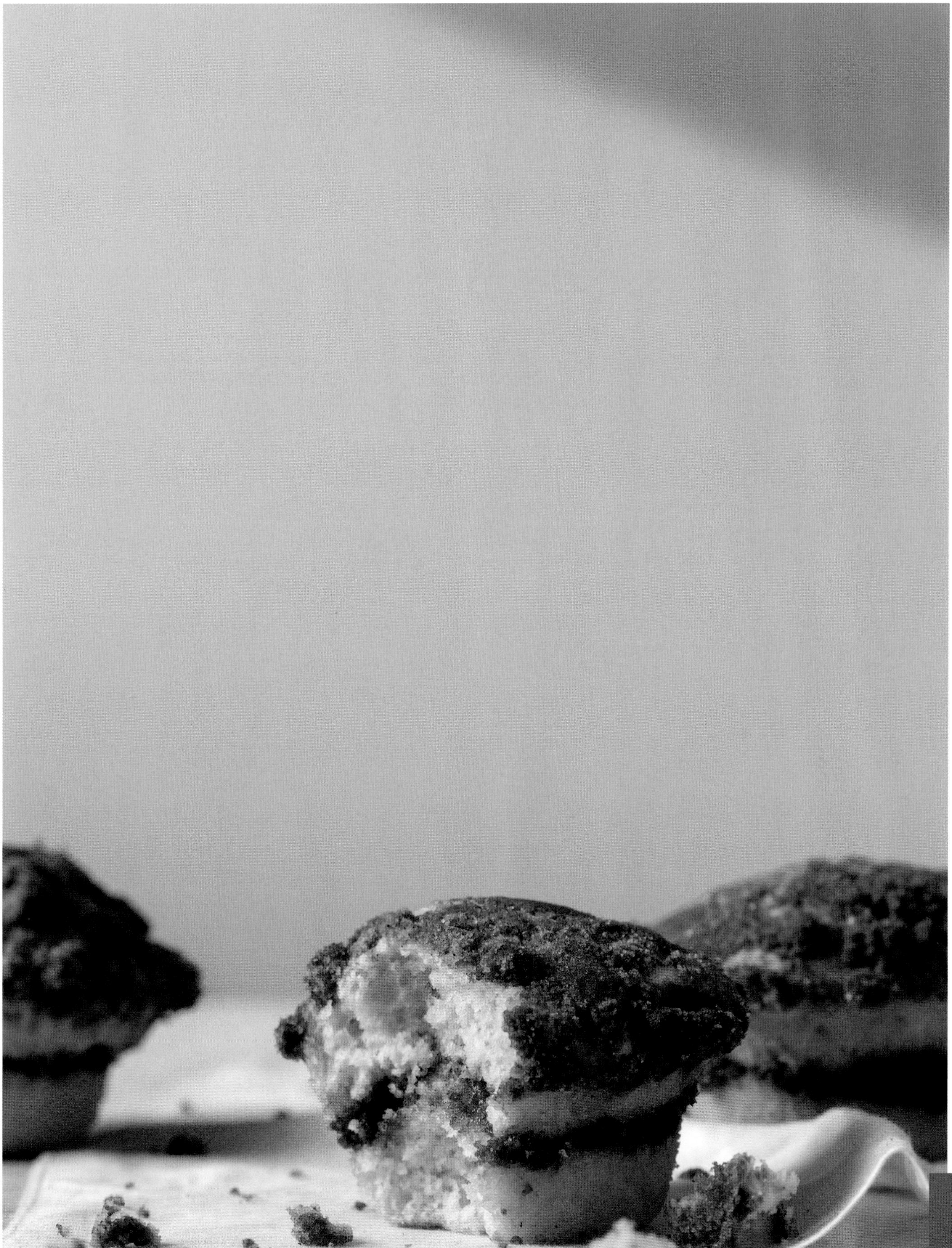

GRANOLA BARS

Pareve **YIELDS** *16 servings*

Searching for a healthy homemade snack or breakfast on the go? Look no further. These granola bars deliver.

3 cups	old-fashioned oats
2½ Tbsp	dark brown sugar
6 Tbsp	wheat germ
¼ cup	unsweetened shredded coconut
⅓ cup	honey
⅓ cup	canola oil
1 Tbsp	water
¾ Tbsp	vanilla extract
½ cup	Rice Krispies
¼ cup	chocolate chips

1. Preheat oven to 300°F. Line a 9x13-inch baking pan with parchment paper.

2. In a large bowl, combine oats, brown sugar, wheat germ, and coconut.

3. In the microwave, in a microwave-safe bowl or cup, warm honey and oil for 30 seconds. Add to oat mixture; mix very well until completely coated. Add water, vanilla, Rice Krispies, and chocolate chips. Mix well until very well coated.

4. Press mixture into prepared pan. Flatten and smooth mixture into an even layer.

5. Bake for 30 minutes.

6. Remove from oven; immediately slice into bars.

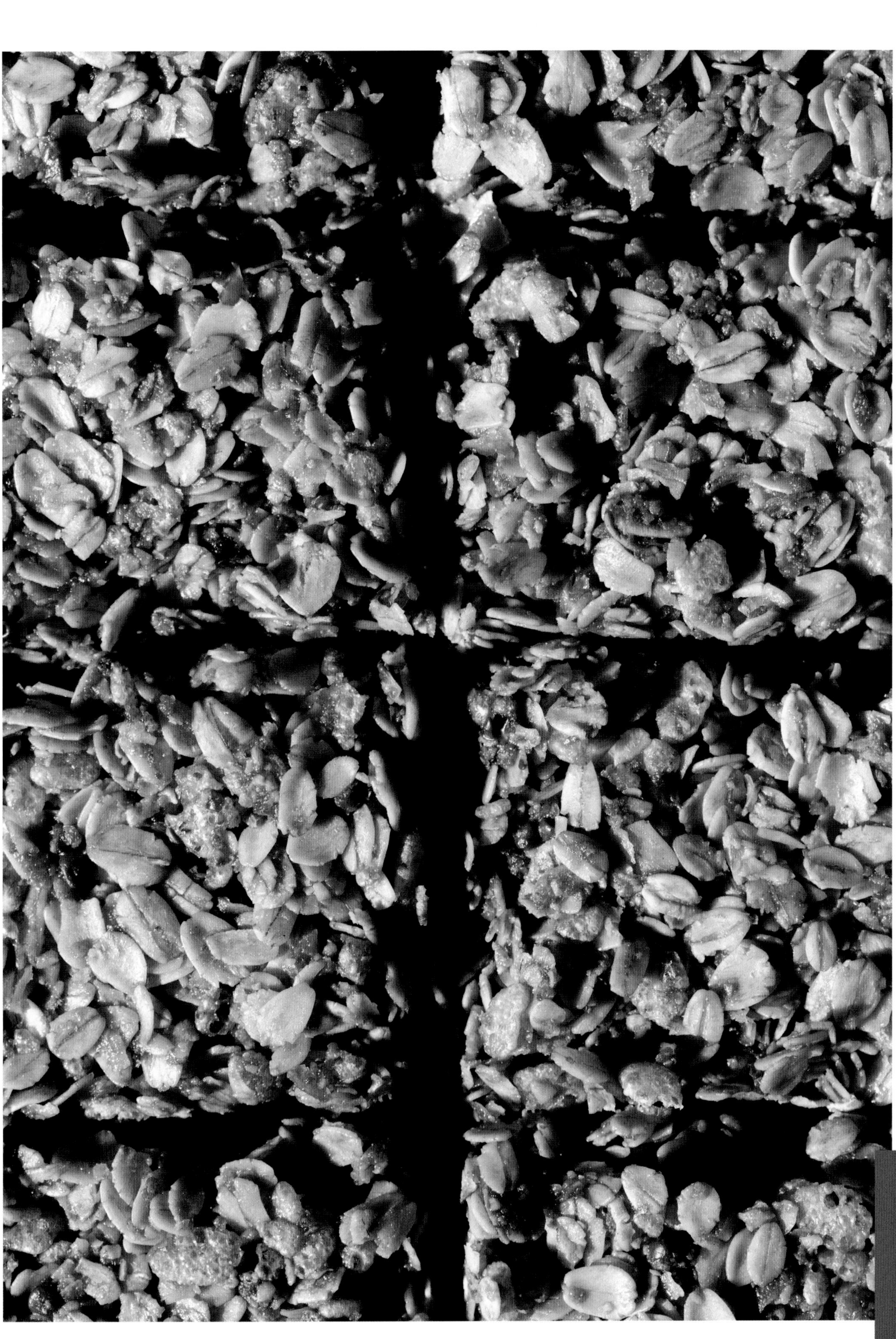

CHOCOLATE BUNS

Pareve **YIELDS** *36-40 buns*

I have searched high and low, and spent years trying, tweaking, and perfecting different combinations of dough, fillings, and methods. I was never completely satisfied until I put together this perfect combination that I know you'll love as much as I do.

Dough

6½ cups	flour, divided
6 Tbsp	sugar
1½ tsp	sea salt
4½ tsp	dry yeast (2 packets)
1 cup	nondairy milk
⅓ cup	margarine
¾ cup	water
3	eggs, room temperature

Chocolate Filling

1½ cups	sugar
1½ cups	powdered sugar
¾ cup	cocoa
3 Tbsp	vanilla sugar
½ cup	canola oil, for smearing

Honey Glaze

½ cup	sugar
4 Tbsp	water
1 Tbsp	honey

Chocolate Drizzle

1¾ cups	powdered sugar
2 Tbsp	nondairy milk
2-3 Tbsp	chocolate liquor
1 tsp	canola oil

—Note—

Glazing the buns is an extra step, but it will lock the moisture into your buns and keep them fresh longer.

This recipe is freezer friendly!

1. **Prepare the dough:** Place 2 cups flour, sugar, salt, and dry yeast into the large bowl of an electric mixer fitted with the dough hook.

2. In a saucepan over medium-low heat, heat milk, margarine, and water until margarine begins to melt. Do not bring to a boil. Pour warm liquid into the mixing bowl; beat for 2 minutes at medium speed. Add eggs and ½ cup flour. Beat for 2 minutes at high speed. Lower speed; beat in remaining 4 cups flour. Dough should not stick to the sides at all (you may sprinkle in a little more flour if necessary). Beat for 8 minutes on medium speed.

3. Place dough into a greased bowl. Grease the top of the dough. Cover; allow to rise until doubled in size, about 1 hour.

4. **Prepare the chocolate filling:** In a medium bowl, stir together sugars, cocoa, and vanilla sugar. Mix until fully incorporated.

5. **Assemble the buns:** Lightly grease and flour 3 (9x13-inch) baking pans. Divide dough into thirds. Roll 1 piece of dough into an 8x12-inch rectangle, on a lightly floured surface. Smear with ⅓ of the oil. Sprinkle with ⅓ filling mixture. Roll tightly, jelly-roll style, lengthwise. Cut into 12 (1-inch) slices. Lay buns into prepared pan 3 across, 4 down, leaving space in between each bun. Repeat with remaining dough segments. Cover; allow to rest 15-20 minutes.

6. Preheat oven to 350°F.

7. Bake for 20 minutes, until lightly golden.

8. **Meanwhile, prepare honey glaze:** Place glaze ingredients into a small saucepan. Bring to a boil. Reduce heat; simmer for 5 minutes (see Note).

9. Remove buns from the oven; brush with glaze.

10. **Prepare the chocolate drizzle:** Whisk together drizzle ingredients. Let rest for 10-15 minutes. Drizzle over cooled buns.

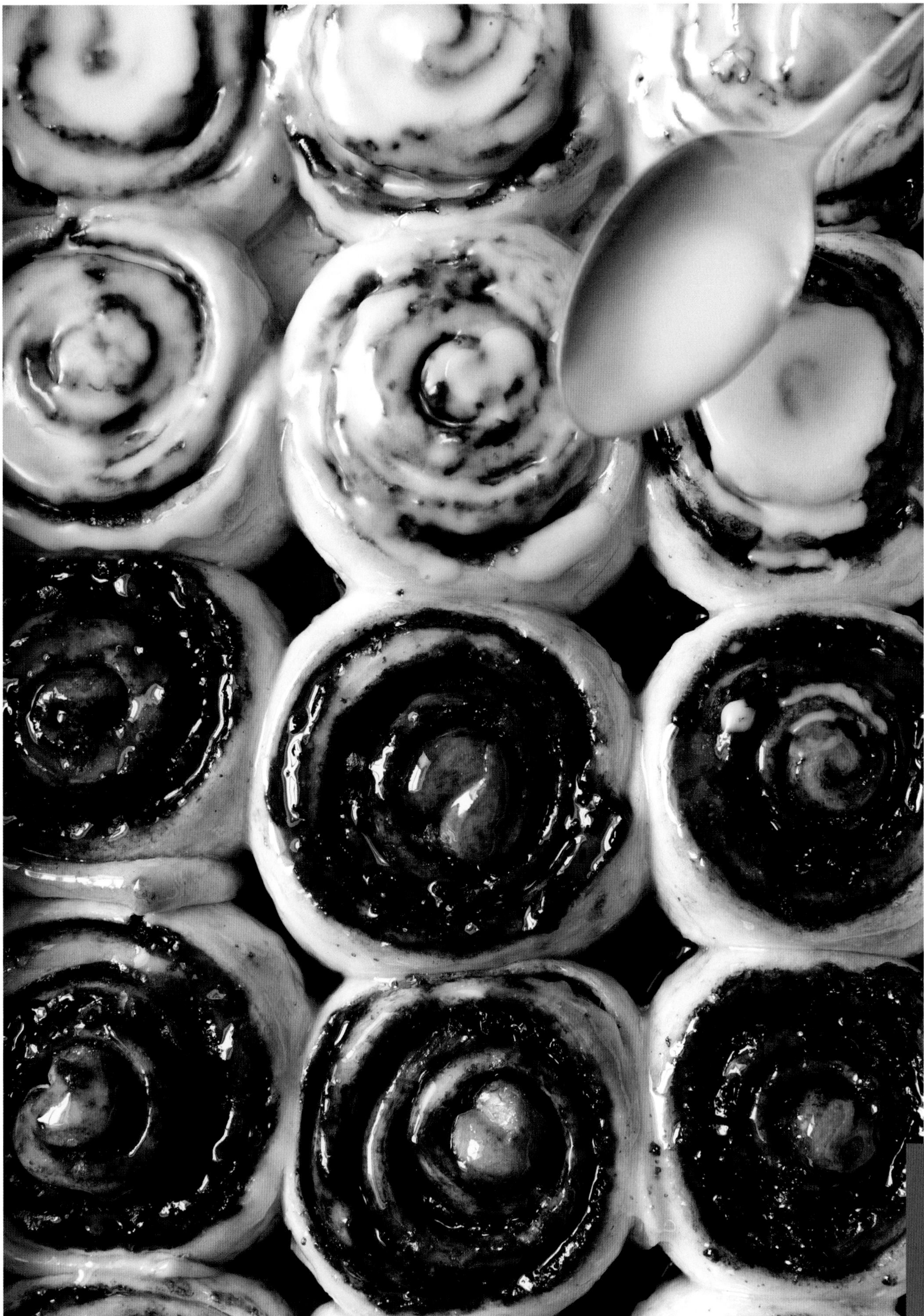

S'MORES RUGELACH

Pareve   **YIELDS** *36 rugelach*

2½ cups	flour
1 tsp	baking powder
¼ cup	sugar
¼ tsp	kosher salt
1 cup (2 sticks)	cold margarine, cubed
½ cup	nondairy milk

S'mores Filling

1 cup	chocolate spread
1 cup	marshmallow crème
1 sleeve	graham crackers (about 10), crushed

Optional Garnish

¼ cup	sugar
1 tsp	vanilla sugar
1 tsp	cocoa
2 oz	quality chocolate, melted

S'mores aren't just to be enjoyed around a campfire. The components of this yeast-free pastry are all of the flavors that go into everyone's favorite s'mores treat. They are delectable on their own, but are even more fun when you turn them into rugelach.

1. In a large bowl, combine flour, baking powder, sugar, and salt. Using a pastry cutter or 2 knives, cut in the cold margarine until mixture is crumbly (can also be mixed by hand). Mix in nondairy milk. Divide the dough into 3 equal portions; shape each into a ball.

2. Preheat oven to 350°F. Grease a baking sheet.

3. Roll 1 ball of dough into a 12-inch circle. Smear with ⅓ cup chocolate spread, then with ⅓ cup marshmallow crème. (You can warm crème in a microwave-safe bowl in the microwave for a few seconds to soften, easing the spreading process.) Sprinkle ⅓ cup graham cracker crumbs over the fluff. Cut into 12 wedges. Roll up wedges from the outer edge to the point. The tighter they are rolled, the prettier the rugelach will be. Repeat these steps with the remaining 2 balls of dough.

4. Place rugelach, point-side down, onto prepared baking sheet; form into crescent shapes.

5. **Optional garnish:** In a small bowl, combine sugar, vanilla sugar, and cocoa. Sprinkle generously over rugelach. Bake 16-18 minutes or until lightly browned. Do not overbake.

6. Allow to cool. If desired, drizzle with melted chocolate.

Note

This recipe is freezer friendly!

BUTTER CRINKLE COOKIES

Dairy **YIELDS** *4 dozen cookies*

½ **cup**	powdered sugar
½ **cup** (1 stick)	butter, chilled
⅓ **cup**	sour cream
1½ **cups**	sugar
1	egg
2 **tsp**	vanilla bean paste *or* vanilla extract
2 **cups**	flour
½ **cup**	dry milk powder, such as Baker's Choice
3 **tsp**	baking powder
¼ **tsp**	sea salt

Crunchy on the outside, chewy on the inside, these cookies are a buttery, dairy delight.

1. Preheat oven to 350°F. Line 3 baking sheets with parchment paper

2. Place powdered sugar into a bowl; set aside.

3. Using an electric mixer, beat together butter, sour cream, and sugar until blended. Do not overbeat. Beat in egg and vanilla. Slowly beat in flour, milk powder, baking powder, and salt.

4. Shape 1 tablespoon of dough in a ball by hand, or use a small scoop. Roll the ball in prepared powdered sugar, coating it completely. Place on prepared baking sheet; repeat with remaining dough. Arrange 4 across and 5 down on each baking sheet.

5. Bake 12-14 minutes. If using disposable baking sheets it will be 14 minutes. If using metal baking sheets it will be 12 minutes, as metal conducts heat more evenly and quickly.

6. Cool before serving.

Note

This recipe is freezer friendly!

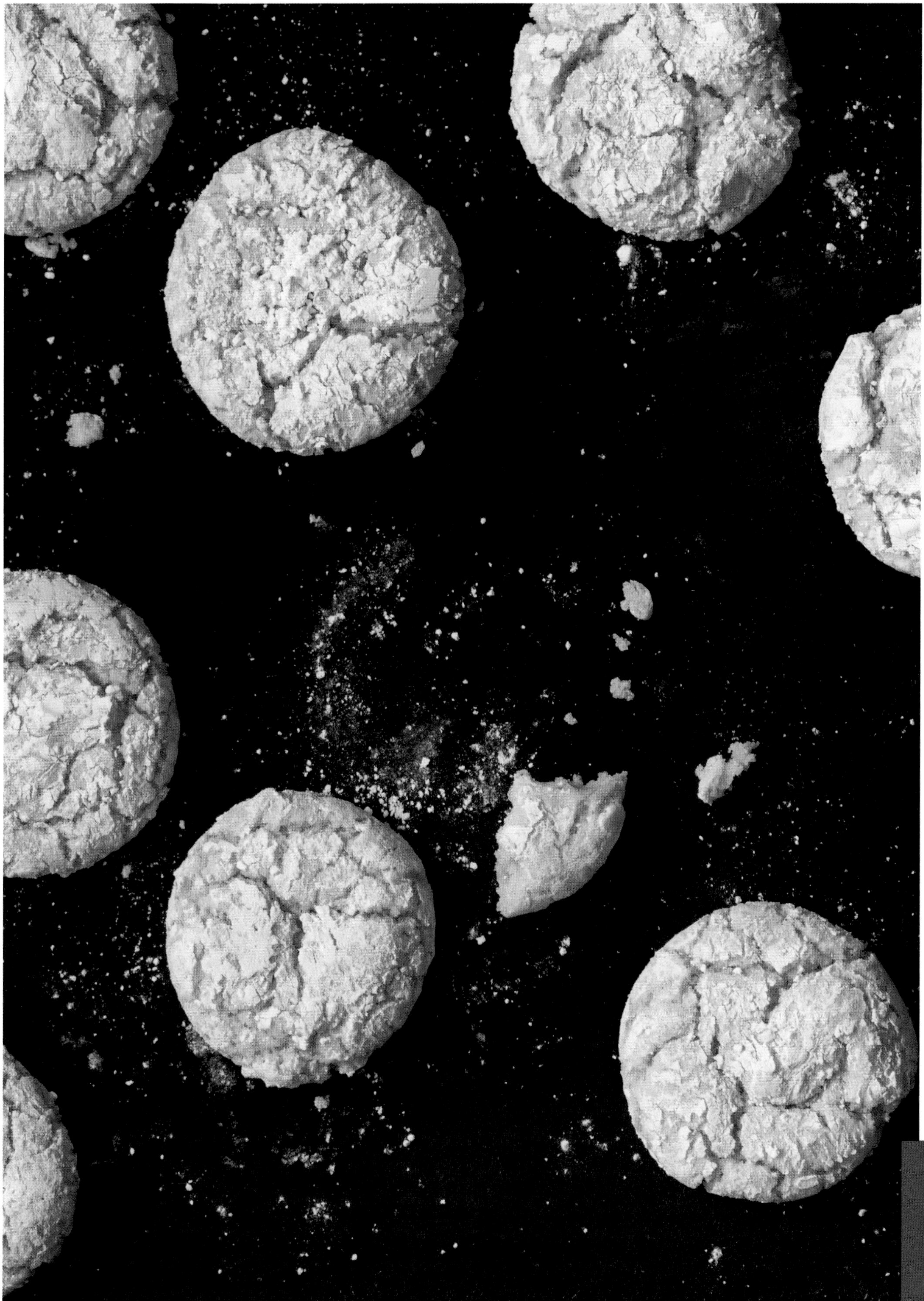

NIGHT & DAY CHOCOLATE CHIP COOKIES

Pareve **YIELDS** *20-24 cookies*

2	eggs
¾ cup	sugar
¾ cup	dark brown sugar, packed
¾ cup + 2 Tbsp	canola oil
1 Tbsp	vanilla extract
2¼ cups	flour
¾ tsp	baking powder
¾ tsp	baking soda
¼ tsp	sea salt

Classic Chocolate Chip Mixture

¼ cup	flour
2 Tbsp	wheat germ
9 oz (1½ cups)	chocolate chunks, divided

Double Chocolate Chip Mixture

5 oz	quality chocolate, broken into small chunks
2 Tbsp	Dutch processed cocoa
9 oz (1½ cups)	chocolate chips, divided

There's nothing like fresh homemade chocolate chip cookies. I love playing around with different ways to change up this classic. Whether you're a chocolate chip or chocolate chocolate chip fan, these will certainly satisfy your cookie cravings.

1. Using an electric mixer fitted with the cookie paddle, combine eggs and sugars. Beat at medium speed for 1 minute, until light and fluffy. Add oil; mix until incorporated. Reduce speed to low; add remaining ingredients and beat until just combined. Scrape the bottom and sides to ensure all ingredients are well incorporated.

2. Remove half the dough; set aside.

3. **Prepare the classic chocolate chip mixture:** Beat additional flour and wheat germ into the remaining batter in the mixer bowl. Transfer to a second bowl. Fold in 1 cup chocolate chunks. Set aside.

4. **Prepare the double chocolate chip mixture:** In a microwave-safe bowl, heat chocolate at 20 second intervals, stirring between each time, until chocolate is just melted. Set aside; allow to cool. Return the reserved cookie dough to the mixer bowl. Add cocoa; beat on low until well blended. Add melted chocolate; beat on low speed until just combined. Fold in 1 cup chocolate chips.

5. Preheat oven to 350°F. Line 2 baking sheets with parchment paper.

6. Use a small scoop or measure how much dough is needed to roll into a 1-inch ball. Prepare a 1-inch ball of classic chocolate chip. Prepare a 1-inch ball of double chocolate chip. Press the 2 balls of dough together; roll into a large ball. Place cookie on prepared baking sheet. Repeat for each cookie. Since these cookies are slightly larger than standard, leave at least 3 inches between cookies. Do not bake more than 8 cookies at a time. (Continues on facing page.)

—**Tip**—

Allow baking sheets to cool completely between batches. You may run sheets under cold water to speed up the process.

—**Note**—

These cookies are freezer friendly.

7. Bake cookies for 8 minutes (rotating sheets halfway if baking 2 sheets simultaneously). Remove baking sheet from the oven. Garnish classic chocolate chip side with a few additional chunks from remaining ½ cup. Garnish double chocolate chip side with a few additional chips from remaining ½ cup. You can slightly press chocolate into the cookie to set it.

8. Return to oven. Bake 1½-2 minutes. Remove baking sheet from oven; cool 3-5 minutes. Transfer to a wire rack to continue to cool completely. Cookies remain fresh, stored in an airtight bag or container for a week.

HONEY CARDAMOM COOKIES

Pareve **YIELDS** *60 cookies*

2¾ cups	flour
2 tsp	baking powder
1 tsp	cinnamon
pinch	ground ginger
½ tsp	sea salt
1 tsp	cardamom
1 large	egg
1 cup	sugar
¾ cup	canola oil
½ cup	honey
1 tsp	vanilla extract
½ cup	turbinado sugar (see Note on page 44), for topping

I have never been a huge fan of honey cookies ... until these. Every bite has fantastic flavor and the right amount of crunch. You won't want to save these just for Rosh Hashanah.

1. Preheat oven to 350°F. Line 3 baking sheets with parchment paper; lightly coat with cooking spray.

2. In a large bowl, combine flour, baking powder, cinnamon, ginger, salt, and cardamom; set aside.

3. Using an electric mixer, beat egg and sugar till light and creamy. Add oil; beat until fully incorporated. Add honey and vanilla; beat until mixture is smooth and creamy.

4. Stir in the flour mixture (do not overbeat). Scoop out one tablespoon of dough and roll into a ball. Then roll in the turbinado sugar. Place on cookie sheet. Flatten cookie with palm. Repeat with remaining dough.

5. Bake for 11–12 minutes. Cool for 1-2 minutes; transfer to a cooling rack.

Note

This recipe is freezer friendly!

SNOWBALL TRUFFLES

Pareve **YIELDS** *38-40 cookies*

My goal in developing these cookies was to create a total melt-in-your-mouth experience. After multiple attempts, this truffle-nestled snowball cookie was born.

Dough

1 cup (2 sticks)	margarine
1 tsp	vanilla extract
¾ cup	powdered sugar
2 cups	flour

Truffles

4 oz	bittersweet quality pareve chocolate, such as Noblesse 54%
2 oz	praline paste
½ cup	powdered sugar, for coating

1. **Prepare the dough:** Using an electric mixer on high speed, cream margarine. Add vanilla and sugar; mix until smooth. Reduce speed to low; add flour, scraping the sides as needed, and mixing until mixture comes together to form a dough.

2. Transfer dough to a piece of parchment paper. Shape dough into 2 (10-inch) logs. Wrap in parchment paper. Refrigerate while preparing the truffles.

3. **Prepare the truffles:** Line a baking sheet with parchment paper.

4. Melt chocolate and praline paste over a double boiler, until completely melted and combined, stirring occasionally. Remove bowl from the double boiler; set aside until cool to touch.

5. Using gloved hands, make small truffle balls the size of a marble, using a 1-teaspoon measuring spoon. Roll each piece between your hands to form a ball; place on prepared cookie sheet. (If your hands get sticky, dust with powdered sugar.) Freeze truffles for 30 minutes to make the wrapping process (see Step 7) easier. If pressed for time, you can continue right away but you may have to dust your hands with powdered sugar as described.

6. Preheat oven to 350°F. Line a baking sheet with parchment paper.

7. Remove dough logs from refrigerator. Slice each into 20 pieces. Roll a piece of dough into a ball; flatten it in the palm of your hand. Place a truffle into the center of dough; wrap dough around truffle to cover completely. Roll into a ball between your hands; seal well. Repeat with remaining dough and truffles, placing wrapped truffles onto prepared baking sheet, 2 inches apart.

8. Bake 18-20 minutes, until lightly colored.

9. Roll hot cookies in powdered sugar. Let cool 10 minutes; roll in sugar again.

— Note

These cookies freeze beautifully.

NO-BAKE CHEESECAKE MELTAWAYS

Dairy

YIELDS *approximately 40 balls*

2 (3½ oz) bars	dairy white chocolate
½ cup (1 stick)	butter, room temperature
1 (8-oz) package	cream cheese, room temperature
2 Tbsp	amaretto *or* Kahlua *or* vanilla vodka
¼ tsp	vanilla extract

Chocolate Coating

2-3 bars (3½-oz)	white or dark chocolate, or use both to create a beautiful effect

These cheesecake bites are surprisingly easy to make. They are so decadent; you won't be able to stop at just one.

1. In the microwave, melt the white chocolate in a microwave-safe bowl at 20-second intervals for about 2 minutes, stirring well until completely smooth. Alternatively, melt chocolate over a double boiler.

2. Using an electric mixer, beat butter and cream cheese until smooth. Add amaretto and vanilla. Beat in melted chocolate. Cover; refrigerate for 1 hour.

3. Line a baking sheet with parchment paper.

4. Remove mixture from refrigerator. Shape into 1-inch balls (I used a small scoop and then rolled by hand). Place onto prepared cookie sheet. Refrigerate for 2 hours until firm.

5. **Prepare the chocolate coating:** In the microwave, melt 2 bars chocolate in a microwave-safe bowl at 20-second intervals for about 2 minutes, stirring well until completely smooth Alternatively, melt chocolate over a double boiler. Stir until smooth.

6. Hold a cheesecake ball in tongs or between a fork and spoon. Dip balls into mixture. Allow excess to drip off. Return to baking sheet.

7. Optional: If you coated your cheesecake bites with dark chocolate, melt half a bar of white chocolate. Transfer melted chocolate to a small resealable bag. Snip a tiny part of corner off. Drizzle over chocolate-covered balls. If you coated the cheesecake balls with white chocolate, drizzle with dark chocolate.

8. Refrigerate until set.

— Note
These cheesecake bites can be frozen for 2 months.

— Tip
For perfectly even balls, use a small scoop and a cup of hot water. Dip the scoop into the hot water between each cheesecake ball.

PISTACHIO SHORTBREAD BISCOTTI

Pareve **YIELDS** *24-30 biscotti*

3	eggs
¾ cup	powdered sugar
½ cup	sugar
1 Tbsp	vanilla sugar
1 cup	canola oil
3½ cups	flour
2 Tbsp	cornstarch
2 tsp	baking powder
¼ tsp	sea salt
½ cup	shelled roasted pistachios, salted or unsalted, chopped

Chocolate Dip

1 cup	semisweet chocolate chips
¼ cup	finely crushed roasted pistachios, salted or unsalted

Shortbread cookies are usually made with butter. These dairy-free biscotti are close to the real thing. They are simple and will satisfy your cookie craving.

1. Preheat oven to 350°F. Line a baking sheet with parchment paper.

2. In an electric mixer fitted with the cookie paddles, on medium speed, cream eggs and sugars until combined. Lower speed; gradually add oil. Return speed to medium; beat until light yellow and fluffy. Turn off mixer; add flour, cornstarch, baking powder, and salt. Slowly pulse until incorporated; beat on low until dough has formed, and the sides of your mixer are clean. Beat in the pistachios.

3. Divide dough into thirds; with wet hands, form into 3 loaves, each about 8 inches long. Place loaves on prepared baking sheet.

4. Bake on center rack for 40 minutes. Cool for 5 minutes; slice. If you enjoy crispier biscotti, turn each slice on its side; bake 2-3 minutes longer. Repeat on second side.

5. **Prepare the chocolate dip:** In a microwave-safe bowl, melt chocolate in the microwave at 20-second intervals, stirring well between. Alternatively, melt over a double boiler.

6. Once biscotti have cooled, dip the corner of each cookie into the chocolate; allow the excess to drip back into bowl. Sprinkle with crushed pistachios. Set aside to dry.

— Note
This recipe is freezer friendly!

INDEX